Michael M. Dediu

Socrates to Churchill
Aphorisms
celebrated after 1960

A chronological and photographic documentary

DERC Publishing House
Tewksbury (Boston), Massachusetts, U. S. A.

Copyright ©2019 by Michael M. Dediu

All rights reserved

Published and printed in the
United States of America
On the Great Seal of the United States (1782) are included:
E Pluribus Unum (Out of many, one) – on the front
Annuit Coeptis (He has approved of the undertakings) – reverse up
Novus Ordo Seclorum (New order of the ages) - on the reverse down, and printed on the back of the one-dollar bill since 1935

Library of Congress Control Number: 2019901138

Dediu, Michael M.

Socrates to Churchill Aphorisms celebrated after 1960
A chronological and photographic documentary

ISBN-13: 978-1-939757-83-8

Preface

Who are the authors of the following aphorisms?

"Without books the development of civilization would have been impossible. They are the engines of change, windows on the world, "Lighthouses" as the poet said "erected in the sea of time." They are companions, teachers, magicians, bankers of the treasures of the mind. Books are humanity in print."

"Books constitute capital."

"A home without books is a body without soul."

"The reading of all good books is like a conversation with the finest minds of past centuries."

"You cannot open a book without learning something."

The answers are here, together with many other famous aphorisms, beautiful pictures, and other information.

This book awaits to be explored - starting from 1960, in a chronological order, many great personalities and their aphorisms are remembered in these last 60 years. There are also many attractive and historic photographs – I want to thank my wife for her great assistance.

This book uses Pythagoras' advice: "Do not say a little in many words, but a great deal in a few. "

Michael M. Dediu, Ph. D.

Tewksbury (Boston), U. S. A., 30 January 2019

Chicago (1833): on the Michigan Avenue Bridge over Chicago River, 333 North Michigan Building (left, 1928, 34 fl, 120 m), Carbide & Carbon Hotel (center-left, 1929, 38 fl, 153 m), London Guarantee Building (center-right, 1923, 22 fl, 97 m), upper part of the Mather Tower (center right up, 1928, 42 fl, 158 m).

Table of Contents

Preface 3

Chapter 1. 1960 - 1969 7

Chapter 2. 1970 - 1979 23

Chapter 3. 1980 - 1989 44

Chapter 4. 1990 - 1999 65

Chapter 5. 2000 - 2009 90

Chapter 6. 2010 - 2019 118

Bibliography 143

Rome (753 BC): Trajan's column (center) was erected in 113 AD in honor of Emperor Trajan (53 - 117, Emperor 98 – 117). It is located at the Forum of Trajan, near Piazza Venezia (from which the picture is taken) and Altare della Patria. The column commemorates Trajan's victories in Dacia (now Romania), and is 42 meters tall. The church Santissimo Nome di Maria al Foro Traiano (1751) is on the left.

Chapter 1. 1960 - 1969

1960

- 2600th anniversary of the birth of **Solon** (640 BC Athens, Greece – 558 BC, Cyprus, aged 82), Athenian statesman, lawmaker and poet, who legislated against political, economic and moral decline in archaic Athens, and thus he laid the foundations for Athenian democracy. Quotes:

I grow old learning something new every day.

Learn to obey before you command.

Laws are the spider's webs which, if anything small falls into them they ensnare it, but large things break through and escape.

Put more trust in nobility of character than in an oath.

In giving advice seek to help, not to please, your friend.

- 1900th anniversary of the birth of **Decimus Iunius Iuvenalis** (known in English as Juvenal, 60, Aquino, Roman Empire – 127, Roma, Roman Empire, aged 67), Roman poet and the author of the collection of satirical poems known as the Satires.

Damna minus consulta movent - Losses to which we are accustomed affect us less deeply.

Mens sana in corpore sano - A sound mind in a sound body.

Difficile est saturam non scribere. - It is hard not to write satire.

Panem et circenses. - Bread and circuses.

Probitas laudatur et alget. - Honesty is praised and left in the cold.

Sed quis custodiet ipsos custodes? - Who watches the watchmen?

Sic volo, sic iubeo. - I want this, I order this.

Nil proeteter nubes, et coeli numen adorant. - Nought but the clouds, and heavens God adores.

- over 2,300 years ago, in Rome a new Latin phrase appears:

Ab uno disce omnes (From one (person/example) **judge the rest (**or learn to know all**).**

1961

- 1900th anniversary of the birth of **Gaius Plinius Caecilius Secundus** (also known as Pliny the Younger, 61, Como, Roman Empire – 113, Bithynia, Roman Empire, aged 52), Roman politician and author. His uncle, Gaius Plinius Secundus, also known as Pliny the Elder, 38 years older, helped raise and educate him until the age of 18, when his uncle died. Quotes:

Multi famam, conscientiam pauci verentur. - Many fear their reputation, few their conscience.

He [Gaius Plinius Secundus or Pliny the Elder] used to say that "no book was so bad, but some good might be got out of it".

However often you may have done them a favor, if you once refuse, they forget everything except your refusal.

An object in possession seldom retains the same charm that it had in pursuit.

- 15 February - 100th anniversary of the birth of **Alfred North Whitehead** (15 February 1861 – 30 December 1947, aged 86.8) OM (Order of Merit (French: Ordre du Mérite)), FRS (Fellowship of the Royal Society), FBA (Fellowship of the British Academy). He was an English mathematician and philosopher. He introduced the philosophical school known as process philosophy, which today has found application to many disciplines, including ecology, theology, education, physics, biology, economics, and psychology. Quote:

Civilizations can only be understood by those who are civilized.

But you can catch yourself entertaining habitually certain ideas and setting others aside; and that, I think, is where our personal destinies are largely decided.

Civilization advances by extending the number of important operations which we can perform without thinking of them.

- over 2,200 years ago, in Rome a new Latin phrase appears:
Natura abhorret a vacuo (Nature abhors a vacuum)

1962

- 23 January - 100th anniversary of the birth of **David Hilbert** (23 Jan 1862 – 14 Feb 1943, aged 81 years and 22 days), important German mathematician. Quote:

No other question has ever moved so profoundly the spirit of man; no other idea has so fruitfully stimulated his intellect; yet no other concept stands in greater need of clarification than that of the infinite.

- over 2,100 years ago, the Romans required:
Nemo iudex in causa sua (No man shall be a judge in his own cause).

Rome (753 BC): Piazza del Quirinale, with a Roman obelisk from Augustus period (27 BC – 14 AD), erected here in 1786 by Pius VII Pontifex Maximus (Supreme Pontiff), between two horse tamers to the left and right, and with a large water bowl in front, placed around 1850.

1963

- 29 January - **Robert Frost** passed away (26 March 1874, San Francisco, CA – 29 Jan 1963, Boston, MA, aged 88.8). He was an American poet influenced by Horatius' "Ars Poetica", initially he published in England, before he was published in America. Known for his realistic depictions of rural life, and his command of American colloquial speech, Frost frequently wrote about settings from rural life in New England, around Boston. Quote:

Education is the ability to listen to almost anything without losing your temper or your self-confidence.

- over 2,300 years ago, in Rome a new Latin expression appears:

Volens nolens (Willing, unwilling = like it or not)

The city Niagara Falls, Ontario, Canada, with its Skylon Tower (center-left, 1965, 160 m, a Revolving Dining Room), and the boarding place (center-right) for the boat to the Horseshoe Falls.

1964

- 15 February - 400th anniversary of the birth of **Galileo Galilei** (15 February 1564 – 8 January 1642, aged 77.9), Italian polymath. Known for his work as a mathematician, astronomer, physicist, engineer, and philosopher, Galileo has been called the "father of observational astronomy", the "father of modern physics", the "father of the scientific method", and the "father of science". Quotes:

In questions of science, the authority of a thousand is not worth the humble reasoning of a single individual.

All truths are easy to understand once they are discovered; the point is to discover them.

I do not feel obliged to believe that the same God, who has endowed us with sense, reason, and intellect, has intended us to forgo their use.

I have never met a man so ignorant that I couldn't learn something from him.

Mathematics is the language with which God has written the universe.

The Sun, with all those planets revolving around it and dependent upon it, can still ripen a bunch of grapes, as if it had nothing else in the universe to do.

- 23 April - 400th anniversary of the birth of **William Shakespeare** (23 April 1564 (baptized on 26 – the only recorded date)—23 April 1616, aged 52, English poet, playwright and actor, widely regarded as the greatest writer in the English language). He was born in Stratford-upon-Avon (130 km northwest of London, and 35 km southeast of Birmingham), Warwickshire, England. Quotes:

Love all, trust a few, do wrong to none.
We know what we are, but know not what we may be.
Women may fall when there's no strength in men.
Better three hours too soon than a minute too late.
Brevity is the soul of wit.

- 20 October – former U.S. President **Herbert Clark Hoover** passed away at age 90.2 (10 Aug 1874 – 20 Oct 1964). He was an American engineer, businessman and politician, who served as the 31st president of the United States from 1929 to 1933. Quotes:

All men are equal before fish.

Freedom is the open window through which pours the sunlight of the human spirit and human dignity.

Older men declare war. But it is youth that must fight and die.

Peace is not made at the council table or by treaties, but in the hearts of men.

Blessed are the young for they shall inherit the national debt.

Children are our most valuable natural resource.

- over 2,400 years ago, in Rome, when some politicians were very dominant, the Romans used the Latin expression:

Respice post te! Hominem te esse memento! (Look behind you! Remember that you are but a man!)

Rome: The east side of the Mausoleum (135-139) of Hadrian (76–138, Emperor 117-138, renamed Castel Sant'Angelo in 600). It was used by the popes as a castle and now is a museum.

1965

- 2500th anniversary of the birth of **Heraclitus of Ephesus** (c. 535 BC Ephesus, Persian Empire – c. 475 BC, Ephesus, Persian Empire, aged c. 60) pre-Socratic Greek philosopher. Quotes:
The only constant is change.
No man ever steps in the same river twice, for it's not the same river and he's not the same man.
Change alone is unchanging.
Good character is not formed in a week or a month. It is created little by little, day by day. Protracted and patient effort is needed to develop good character.

- 30 May - 700th anniversary of the birth of **Dante Alighieri** (30 May 1265, Firenze, Italy – 14 Sep 1321, Ravenna, Italy, aged 56.3), great Renaissance poet. Quotes:
Lasciate ogne speranza, voi ch'entrate. - All hope abandon, ye who enter in.
Necessità 'l ci 'nduce, e non diletto. - Necessity brings him here, not pleasure.
Bene ascolta chi la nota. - He listens well who takes notes.
La dimanda onesta
si de' seguir con l'opera tacendo.
A fair request should be followed by the deed in silence.
Libertà va cercando, ch'è sì cara,
come sa chi per lei vita rifiuta.
He goes seeking liberty, which is so dear, as he knows who for it renounces life.
Puro e disposto a salire a le stelle. - Pure and disposed to mount unto the stars.
L'esperîenza
di questa dolce vita.
The experience of this sweet life.
L'amor che muove il sole e l'altre stelle. - The Love which moves the Sun and the other stars.

- 24 January - Sir **Winston Leonard Spencer-Churchill** passed away at age 90.1 (30 Nov 1874 – 24 Jan 1965), He was a British politician, army officer, and writer, who was Prime Minister of the United Kingdom from 1940 to 1945, and again from 1951 to 1955. As Prime Minister, Churchill led Britain to victory in the Second World War. Quotes:

A joke is a very serious thing.

A lie gets halfway around the world before the truth has a chance to get its pants on.

A man does what he must - in spite of personal consequences, in spite of obstacles and dangers and pressures - and that is the basis of all human morality.

A pessimist sees the difficulty in every opportunity; an optimist sees the opportunity in every difficulty.

A politician needs the ability to foretell what is going to happen tomorrow, next week, next month, and next year. And to have the ability afterwards to explain why it didn't happen.

There is no such thing as public opinion. There is only published opinion.

The inherent vice of capitalism is the unequal sharing of blessings; the inherent vice of socialism is the equal sharing of miseries.

All the great things are simple, and many can be expressed in a single word: freedom, justice, honor, duty, mercy, hope.

Attitude is a little thing that makes a big difference.

Courage is what it takes to stand up and speak; courage is also what it takes to sit down and listen.

Criticism may not be agreeable, but it is necessary. It fulfils the same function as pain in the human body. It calls attention to an unhealthy state of things.

If the human race wishes to have a prolonged and indefinite period of material prosperity, they have only got to behave in a peaceful and helpful way toward one another.

If we open a quarrel between past and present, we shall find that we have lost the future.

If you go on with this nuclear arms race, all you are going to do is make the rubble bounce.

Eating words has never given me indigestion.

If you have ten thousand regulations you destroy all respect for the law.

I'm just preparing my impromptu remarks.

I am prepared to meet my Maker. Whether my Maker is prepared for the great ordeal of meeting me is another matter.

- over 2,100 years ago, in Rome, when an orator or politician had a leap in logic, by which a necessary part of an explanation was omitted, the Romans used the Latin expression:
Saltus in demonstrando (Leap in explaining)

Rome (753 BC), Vatican (1929): the Basilica di San Pietro (1506 – 1626,), with the bronze door (center) by Antonio Averulino (1445).

London, Parliament Square, the bronze statue (1973) of Sir Winston Churchill (1874-1965, Prime Minister 1940-1945, 1951-1955 (as Prime Minister he lived at 10 Downing Street, just 400 m northwest (right) from this place; as Churchill's youngest daughter, Mary Soames (1922-2014) had the run of 10 Downing Street, and helped arrange dinner with Stalin (1878-1953) in Moscow, 1942), created by the British sculptor Ivor Roberts-Jones (1913-1996).

1966

- 2500 years ago, in 534 BC, theatre was born in Athens. A priest of Dionysus (a god of fertility and wine in Greece), by the name of Thespis, engages in a dialogue with the chorus, becoming the first actor. Thespis is also the first winner of a theatrical award. He takes the prize in the first competition for tragedy, held in Athens in 534 BC.

- over 2,200 years ago, in Rome, when an orator or politician had a complicated and unclear speech, the Romans disapproved with the Latin expression:
Sancta simplicitas (Sacred simplicity)

Japan, Osaka (645 AD, the 3rd largest city in Japan, capital of Osaka Prefecture on the main island Honshu): detail of Toyosaki shrine (1772, with the Emperor Kotoku and others enshrined here).

1967

- 15 May - 400th anniversary of the birth of **Claudio Monteverdi** (15 May 1567 – 29 Nov 1643, aged 76.5, great Italian composer). Quotes:
Music is spiritual. The music business is not.
The end of all good music is to affect the soul.
The modern composer builds upon the foundation of truth.

- over 2,300 years ago, in Rome, when the Romans wanted to say that something (like love) is forever, they used the Latin expression:
Seculo seculorum (Forever and ever)

Niagara Falls (8000 BC, the highest flow rate in the world), with the American Falls (left, USA, 21-30 m drop, 290 m wide), the Bridal Veil Falls (center, USA, 21 m drop, 10 m wide) and the Horseshoe Falls (center-right, in Canada, 53 m drop, 790 m wide).

Trieste - 23 Oct 2009, inside Teatro Verdi, commemoration dedicated to Claudio Monteverdi (1567-1643, composer, gambist, singer, and Catholic priest). He wrote 9 books of Madrigali (1587-1643, the ninth book was published posthumously in 1651), 18 operas, but only L'Orfeo (1609), Il ritorno d'Ulisse in patria (1640), L'incoronazione di Poppea (1642), and the famous aria, Lamento, from his second opera L'Arianna (1608), have survived, and sacred music (Vespro della Beata Vergine (1610), Messa in illo tempore (1610), Mass of Thanksgiving (1631), Messa a 4 da Cappela(1641), and others). Monteverdi developed two styles of composition – the heritage of Renaissance polyphony and the new basso continuo technique of the Baroque. He wrote one of the earliest operas, *L'Orfeo that* is the earliest surviving opera still regularly performed.

1968

- 2400 years ago, in 432 BC, the building of the Parthenon in Athens was completed, after 15 years of work (classical temple in Athens, Greece, 447 BC – 432 BC, height 13.72 m, 69.5 m by 30.9 m)

- over 2,300 years ago, in Rome, when the Romans wanted to understand why things may be happening, sometimes contrary to expectations, they used the Latin expression:
Sequere pecuniam (Follow the money)

Chicago (1833): above entrance decorations of the Tribune Tower (1925, 36 floors, 141 m, for Chicago Tribune (1847)), with stones from famous places around the world, and from the Moon, including Harvard University, Arc de Triomph, Switzerland, Great Wall, Parthenon, Taj Mahal, Notre-Dame, and St. Peter's Basilica.

1969

- 15 August: 200th anniversary of the birth of **Napoleone di Buonaparte** (15 Aug 1769, Corsica, France – 5 May 1821, Longwood House, Saint Helena Island, England, aged 51.7, after being, as Napoléon, Emperor of the French for 9.9 years, King of Italy for 9 years, Protector of the Confederation of the Rhine (Germany) for 7.2 years, First Consul of France for 4.5 years).

Quotes:

A leader is a dealer in hope.

A picture is worth a thousand words.

An army marches on its stomach.

In order to govern, the question is not to follow out a more or less valid theory but to build with whatever materials are at hand. The inevitable must be accepted and turned to advantage.

In politics stupidity is not a handicap.

Let the path be open to talent.

Music is the voice that tells us that the human race is greater than it knows.

Never ascribe to malice that which is adequately explained by incompetence.

Nothing is more difficult, and therefore more precious, than to be able to decide.

Soldiers generally win battles; generals get credit for them.

Take time to deliberate, but when the time for action has arrived, stop thinking and go in.

The battlefield is a scene of constant chaos. The winner will be the one who controls that chaos, both his own and the enemy's.

The best way to keep one's word is not to give it.

The first virtue in a soldier is endurance of fatigue; courage is only the second virtue.

The French complain of everything, and always.

- 100 years ago, in 1869, The Boston Musical Instrument Company began to engrave

Ne plus ultra

on its instruments, until 1928, to signify that none were better. Also used:

nec plus ultra or **non plus ultra** (**nothing more beyond**)

It is a descriptive phrase meaning the best or the most extreme example of something.

Rome (753 BC), Vatican City State (1929): interior of the Basilica di San Pietro (1506 – 1626), the tomb of Pope Pius VII (1742 – 1823, Pope 1800 – 1823, attended the Coronation of Napoleon).

Chapter 2. 1970 - 1979

1970

- 2450th anniversary of the birth of Gautama Buddha (c. 480 BC, Lumbini, Nepal – c. 400 BC, Kushinagar, India, aged c. 80) or simply the Buddha (translates "one who is awake"), was a monk, sage, and Teacher on whose teachings Buddhism was founded. Quotes:

Holding on to anger is like grasping a hot coal with the intent of throwing it at someone else; you are the one who gets burned.

However many holy words you read, however many you speak, what good will they do you if you do not act on upon them?

Three things cannot be long hidden: the Sun, the Moon, and the truth.

Better than a thousand hollow words, is one word that brings peace.

17 December – 200th anniversary of the birth of **Ludwig van Beethoven** (baptized 17 December 1770 – 26 March 1827, aged 56.2), great German composer and pianist. Quote:

Music is the wine which inspires one to new generative processes, and I am Bacchus who presses out this glorious wine for mankind, and makes them spiritually drunken.

Recommend to your children virtue; that alone can make them happy, not gold. I speak from experience.

Beethoven can write music, thank God, but he can do nothing else on Earth.

Nothing is more intolerable than to have to admit to yourself your own errors.

There are not barriers erected, which can say to aspiring talents and industry, "Thus far and no farther."

This is the mark of a really admirable man: steadfastness in the face of trouble.

Tones sound, and roar and storm about me until I have set them down in notes.

Paris - The central part of the façade of L'Opéra de Paris (1875): composers Daniel Auber (1782–1871, left), Ludwig van Beethoven (1770–1827, second), Wolfgang Amadeus Mozart (1756–1791, center) and Gaspare Spontini (1774–1851, right).

- 9 November - **Charles de Gaulle** passed away (22 Nov 1890 – 9 Nov 1970, aged 79.9, 13 days before 80), French army officer and statesman who led the French Resistance against Nazi Germany in World War II, and was President of France for 10.2 years. Quotes:

A true leader always keeps an element of surprise up his sleeve, which others cannot grasp but which keeps his public excited and breathless.

Authority doesn't work without prestige, or prestige without distance.

Hearing Mass is the ceremony I most favor during my travels. Church is the only place where someone speaks to me, and I do not have to answer back.

Deliberation is the work of many men. Action, of one alone.

Diplomats are useful only in fair weather. As soon as it rains, they drown in every drop.

Faced with crisis, the man of character falls back on himself. He imposes his own stamp of action, takes responsibility for it, makes it his own.

I have come to the conclusion that politics are too serious a matter to be left to the politicians.

I have heard your views. They do not harmonize with mine. The decision is taken unanimously.

In order to become the master, the politician poses as the servant.

In politics it is necessary either to betray one's country or the electorate. I prefer to betray the electorate.

Nothing great will ever be achieved without great men, and men are great only if they are determined to be so.

One does not arrest Voltaire.

Since a politician never believes what he says, he is quite surprised to be taken at his word.

To govern is always to choose among disadvantages.

Treaties, you see, are like girls and roses; they last while they last.

When I am right, I get angry. Churchill gets angry when he is wrong. We are angry at each other much of the time.

When I want to know what France thinks, I ask myself.

- over 2,400 years ago, in Rome, when the Romans wanted to write a letter, a common beginning was one of the Latin expressions:

Si vales valeo (SVV) (If you are well, I am well)

Si vales bene est ego valeo (SVBEEV) (If you are well, that is good; I am well")

1971

26 April - 1850ᵗʰ anniversary of the birth of **Marcus Aurelius** (26 April 121, Roma, Roman Empire – 17 March 180, Vindobona, Roman Empire, aged 58.9, called the Philosopher), Roman Emperor for 19 years, from 161 to 180. He was the last of the Six Good Emperors (the founder Augustus (27 BC – 14 AD, 40.6 years), then 82 years not so good, then, for 84 years, five consecutive good Emperors: Nerva (96 – 98, 2 years), Trajan (98 – 117, 19 years), Hadrian (117 – 138, 21 years), Antonius Pius (138 – 161, 23 years) and Marcus Aurelius (161 – 180, 19 years)). Quotes:

A man's worth is no greater than his ambitions.

Because a thing seems difficult for you, do not think it is impossible for anyone to accomplish.

When you arise in the morning, think of what a precious privilege it is to be alive - to breathe, to think, to enjoy, to love.

You have power over your mind - not outside events. Understand this, and you will find strength.

Waste no more time arguing about what a good man should be. Be one.

If it is not right, do not do it; if it is not true, do not say it.

Everything we hear is an opinion, not a fact. Everything we see is a perspective, not the truth.

Very little is needed to make a happy life; it is all within yourself, in your way of thinking.

The universe is change; our life is what our thoughts make it.

Each day provides its own gifts.

He who lives in harmony with himself, lives in harmony with the universe.

- 27 December - 400ᵗʰ anniversary of the birth of **Johannes Kepler** (27 December 1571, Weil der Stadt, Germany – 15 November 1630, Regensburg, Germany, aged 58.9), German mathematician, astronomer and philosopher, best known for his laws of planetary motion, and his books Astronomia nova,

Harmonices Mundi, and Epitome Astronomiae Copernicanae. Quotes:

Nature uses as little as possible of anything.

I demonstrate by means of philosophy that the Earth is round, and is inhabited on all sides; that it is insignificantly small, and is borne through the stars.

Planets move in ellipses with the Sun at one focus.

The diversity of the phenomena of nature is so great, and the treasures hidden in the heavens so rich, precisely in order that the human mind shall never be lacking in fresh nourishment.

Truth is the daughter of time, and I feel no shame in being her midwife.

I much prefer the sharpest criticism of a single intelligent man, to the thoughtless approval of the masses.

The radius vector describes equal areas in equal times.

The squares of the periodic times are to each other as the cubes of the mean distances.

- over 2,100 years ago, in Rome appeared he Latin expression:

silentium est aureum (Silence is golden)

Also, **silentium est aurum** (silence is gold).

1972

- 27 December – 150th anniversary of the birth of **Louis Pasteur** (27 December 1822 – 28 September 1895, aged 72.7), French biologist, microbiologist and chemist, renowned for his discoveries of the principles of vaccination, microbial fermentation, and pasteurization. He is remembered for his remarkable breakthroughs in the causes and prevention of diseases, and his discoveries have saved many lives ever since. Quotes:

In the field of scientific observation, chance favors only the prepared mind.

It is surmounting difficulties that makes heroes.

Science knows no country, because knowledge belongs to humanity, and is the torch which illuminates the world. Science is the highest personification of the nation because that nation will remain the first which carries the furthest the works of thought and intelligence.

The universe is asymmetric and I am persuaded that life, as it is known to us, is a direct result of the asymmetry of the universe or of its indirect consequences.

There are no such things as applied sciences, only applications of science.

It does not exist a category of science to which one can give the name applied science. There are science and the applications of science, bound together as the fruit of the tree which bears it.

- 4 July – 196th anniversary of the U. S. Independence Day, and the 100th anniversary of the birth of **John Calvin Coolidge Jr**. (4 July 1872 – 5 Jan 1933, aged 60.5), the 30th President of the United States for 5.6 years, from 2 Aug 1923 (age 51) to 4 March 1929 (age 56.6). On 16 August 1928 (age 56.1) President Coolidge said:

"It is accordance with our determination to refrain from aggression, and build up a sentiment and practice among nations more favorable to peace…that we have incurred the consent of fourteen important nations to the negotiations of a

treaty condemning recourse to war, renouncing it as an instrument of national policy."

The National Museum of the United States Air Force (1923, Dayton, Ohio, the world's largest and oldest military aviation museum): Focke-Wulf Fw 190D-9 (left, small, 1939-1944) and Lockheed P-38 "Lightning" (big, right, 1939-1945).

1973

- 7 May - 2400th anniversary of the birth of **Plato** (7 May 427 BC – 347 BC, aged 80), great Greek philosopher, student of Socrates (43 years older than Plato), teacher of Aristotle (43 years younger than Plato), the founder of the Academy in Athens, the first institution of higher learning in the world. Plato's quotes:

Access to power must be confined to those who are not in love with it.

Any man may easily do harm, but not every man can do good to another.

Excess generally causes reaction, and produces a change in the opposite direction, whether it be in the seasons, or in individuals, or in governments.

A hero is born among a hundred, a wise man is found among a thousand, but an accomplished one might not be found even among a hundred thousand men.

All the gold which is under or upon the earth is not enough to give in exchange for virtue.

And what, Socrates, is the food of the soul? Surely, I said, knowledge is the food of the soul.

Without effort, you cannot be prosperous. Though the land be good, you cannot have an abundant crop without cultivation.

Astronomy compels the soul to look upwards, and leads us from this world to another.

At the touch of love everyone becomes a poet.

Attention to health is life's greatest hindrance.

Courage is knowing what not to fear.

Democracy passes into despotism.

Democracy... is a charming form of government, full of variety and disorder; and dispensing a sort of equality to equals and unequals alike.

Dictatorship naturally arises out of democracy, and the most aggravated form of tyranny and slavery out of the most extreme liberty.

Every heart sings a song, incomplete, until another heart whispers back.

Those who wish to sing always find a song.

For a man to conquer himself is the first and noblest of all victories.

For good nurture and education implant good constitutions.

Good actions give strength to ourselves and inspire good actions in others.

Good people do not need laws to tell them to act responsibly, while bad people will find a way around the laws.

He who commits injustice is ever made more wretched than he who suffers it.

Human behavior flows from three main sources: desire, emotion, and knowledge.

I exhort you also to take part in the great combat, which is the combat of life, and greater than every other earthly conflict.

If particulars are to have meaning, there must be universals.

Let parents bequeath to their children not riches, but the spirit of reverence.

Love is the joy of the good, the wonder of the wise, the amazement of the Gods.

Man - a being in search of meaning.

Music is a moral law. It gives soul to the universe, wings to the mind, flight to the imagination, and charm and gaiety to life and to everything.

Music is the movement of sound to reach the soul for the education of its virtue.

Necessity... the mother of invention.

No man should bring children into the world who is unwilling to persevere to the end in their nature and education.

One of the penalties for refusing to participate in politics is that you end up being governed by your inferiors.

Our object in the construction of the state is the greatest happiness of the whole, and not that of any one class.

Philosophy begins in wonder.

Rhetoric is the art of ruling the minds of men.

The excessive increase of anything causes a reaction in the opposite direction.

The greatest wealth is to live content with little.

The learning and knowledge that we have, is, at the most, but little compared with that of which we are ignorant.

The measure of a man is what he does with power.

The most virtuous are those who content themselves with being virtuous without seeking to appear so.

The punishment which the wise suffer who refuse to take part in the government, is to live under the government of worse men.

There are three classes of men; lovers of wisdom, lovers of honor, and lovers of gain.

There are two things a person should never be angry at, what they can help, and what they cannot

There is no harm in repeating a good thing.

There's a victory, and defeat; the first and best of victories, the lowest and worst of defeats which each man gains or sustains at the hands not of another, but of himself.

This and no other is the root from which a tyrant springs; when he first appears he is a protector.

Those who intend on becoming great should love neither themselves nor their own things, but only what is just, whether it happens to be done by themselves or others.

To love rightly is to love what is orderly and beautiful in an educated and disciplined way.

Truth is the beginning of every good to the gods, and of every good to man.

We can easily forgive a child who is afraid of the dark; the real tragedy of life is when men are afraid of the light

We ought to fly away from earth to heaven as quickly as we can; and to fly away is to become like God, as far as this is possible; and to become like him is to become holy, just, and wise.

When a Benefit is wrongly conferred, the author of the Benefit may often be said to injure.

When the tyrant has disposed of foreign enemies by conquest or treaty, and there is nothing more to fear from them, then he is always stirring up some war or other, in order that the people may require a leader.

When there is an income tax, the just man will pay more and the unjust less on the same amount of income.

Wise men speak because they have something to say; Fools because they have to say something.

- 1950th anniversary of the birth of **Gaius Plinius Secundus** (23 – 25 August 79, aged 56, sometimes called Pliny the Elder). He was a Roman author, naturalist and natural philosopher, an officer of the early Roman Empire, and friend of emperor (who was 14 years older than him, and died 2 months and 2 days before him) Titus Flavius Vespasianus (17 Nov 9 – 23 June 79, aged 69.6, emperor for 10 years: 69 – 79; he started the splendid Amphitheatrum Flavium, which was finished by his son in 80 (now wrongly called Colosseum)). Plinius is the author of the Latin phrase

In vino veritas (In wine [there is the] truth).

There is a similar Greek phrase, which is attributed to the Greek poet Alcaeus of Mytilene (621 BC – 560 BC, aged 61), being the oldest known source for the phrase. The Roman historian Publius Cornelius Tacitus (55 – 117, aged 62) described how the Germanic peoples always drank wine while holding councils, as they believed nobody could lie effectively when drunk.

The phrase is often continued as

In vino veritas, in aqua sanitas (In wine there is truth, in water there is health).

Other Plinius Secundus' quotes

Cum grano salis - With a grain of salt (or wit).

Difficile est tenere quae acceperis nisi exerceas – It is difficult to retain what you may have learned, unless you practice it.

Nemo mortalium omnibus horis sapit – No mortal is wise at all times.

Nulla dies sine linea – Not a day without a line.

- 19 June - 350th anniversary of the birth of **Blaise Pascal** (19 June 1623 – 19 August 1662, aged 39 years and 2 months), important French mathematician, physicist, inventor, and writer. He was a child prodigy, who was educated by his father. Quotes:

It is not certain that everything is uncertain.

Since we cannot know all that there is to be known about anything, we ought to know a little about everything.

Love has reasons which reason cannot understand.
The heart has its reasons that the mind knows nothing of.

Rome (753 BC), Vatican (1929): Piazza di San Pietro (1656 – 1667, Bernini) with Moderno's façade (115 m wide, 46 m high) of the Basilica di San Pietro (1506 – 1626), with 13 statues. Christ, 11 of the Apostles and John the Baptist.

1974

- 22 April - 250th anniversary of the birth of **Immanuel Kant** (22 April 1724 – 12 February 1804, aged 79.8, German philosopher who is a central figure in modern philosophy). Quotes:

Experience without theory is blind, but theory without experience is mere intellectual play.

A categorical imperative would be one which represented an action as objectively necessary in itself, without reference to any other purpose.

All our knowledge begins with the senses, proceeds then to the understanding, and ends with reason. There is nothing higher than reason.

All the interests of my reason, speculative as well as practical, combine in the three following questions: 1. What can I know? 2. What ought I to do? 3. What may I hope?

But although all our knowledge begins with experience, it does not follow that it arises from experience.

By a lie, a man... annihilates his dignity as a man.

Happiness is not an ideal of reason, but of imagination.

Ingratitude is the essence of vileness.

Intuition and concepts constitute... the elements of all our knowledge, so that neither concepts without an intuition in some way corresponding to them, nor intuition without concepts, can yield knowledge.

It is not necessary that whilst I live I live happily; but it is necessary that so long as I live I should live honorably.

Science is organized knowledge. Wisdom is organized life.

- over 2,300 years ago, in Rome, when the Romans wanted to postpone a project for some unknown day in the future, they used the Latin expression:

Sine die (Without a day)

1975

- 2500th anniversary of the birth of **Aeschylus** (c. 525 BC – 456 BC, aged 69), ancient Greek tragedian, who is the father of tragedy. The Oresteia is his only surviving trilogy of ancient Greek plays, which was first performed two years before his death, in 458 BC. Quotes:

In war, truth is the first casualty.
Happiness is a choice that requires effort at times.
It is in the character of very few men to honor, without envy, a friend who has prospered.
Time, as he grows old, teaches all things.
It is always in season for old men to learn.
By Time and Age full many things are taught.
Everyone's quick to blame the alien.

- 2300th anniversary of the birth of **Euclid** (325 BC – 265 BC, aged 60). Great Greek mathematician, the father of geometry. Quotes:

The laws of nature are but the mathematical thoughts of God.
There is no royal road to geometry.

- 6 March – 500th anniversary of the birth of **Michelangelo** di Lodovico Buonarroti Simoni or Michelangelo (6 March 1475, Caprese (20 km northeast of Arezzo, 40 km north of Cortona, 60 km southeast of Firenze) – 18 February 1564, aged 88.9 (just 16 days before 89)), great Italian sculptor, painter, and architect. Quotes:

I saw the angel in the marble and carved until I set him free.
A man paints with his brains and not with his hands.
Every block of stone has a statue inside it, and it is the task of the sculptor to discover it.
I hope that I may always desire more than I can accomplish.
It is well with me only when I have a chisel in my hand.

The greater danger for most of us lies not in setting our aim too high and falling short; but in setting our aim too low, and achieving our mark.

The more the marbles wastes, the more the statue grows.
There is no greater harm than that of time wasted.

Rome (753 BC), Vatican City State (1929): the south-eastern part of the nave of the Basilica di San Pietro (1506 – 1626,), designed by Michelangelo and finished by Maderno, with a Holy Water basin having two cherubs (2 m) who flutter against the first pier.

1976

- 2600th anniversary of the birth of the first mathematician and philosopher - **Thales of Miletus** (c. 624 BC – 547 BC, aged 77), 54 years older than Pythagoras, and Thales died when Pythagoras was 23. Thales' theorem, which states that if A, B and C are points on a circle, where the line AC is a diameter of the circle, then the angle ABC is a right angle.

- 100 years ago, in 1876, Pierre-Auguste Renoir, known as **Auguste Renoir**, 35, (25 February 1841 – 3 December 1919, aged 78.8, French painter) painted Girl with Sheaf of Corn.

- The author, 33, published his first review in the Mathematical Reviews of the American Mathematical Society, of an article published this year, regarding certain structure manifolds.

Niagara Falls (8000 BC, the highest flow rate in the world), with the American Falls (left, USA, 21-30 m drop, 290 m wide), the Bridal Veil Falls (center-left, USA, 21 m drop, 10 m wide) and the Horseshoe Falls (center, in Canada, 53 m drop, 790 m wide).

Girl with Sheaf of Corn by Auguste Renoir, 35, 1876, (25 February 1841 – 3 December 1919, aged 78.8, French painter).

1977

- 1500th anniversary of the birth of **Anicius Manlius Severinus Boëthius** (477, Rome, Italy – 524, Pavia, Italy, aged 47, usually called Boethius), Roman senator, consul, magister officiorum, and influential philosopher. Boëthius' quotes:
Si tacuisses, philosophus mansisses (Latin - If you had been silent, you would have remained a philosopher, or "If you had kept your silence, you would have stayed a philosopher", or "If you'd kept your mouth shut, we might have thought you were clever").
**Nunc fluens facit tempus,
nunc stans facit aeternitatum.**
The now that passes produces time, the now that remains produces eternity.
A man content to go to heaven alone, will never go to heaven.
One's virtue is all that one truly has, because it is not imperiled by the vicissitudes of fortune.

- 30 April – 200th anniversary of the birth of **Johann Carl Friedrich Gauss** (30 April 1777 – 23 February 1855, aged 77 years 9 months and 23 days, of a heart attack, in Göttingen, Kingdom of Hanover (now Lower Saxony, Germany)), German mathematician and physicist who made significant contributions to many fields, including algebra, analysis, astronomy, differential geometry, electrostatics, geodesy, geophysics, magnetic fields, matrix theory, mechanics, number theory, optics and statistics. Referred to as the Princeps mathematicorum (Latin for "the foremost of mathematicians") and "the greatest mathematician since antiquity", Gauss had an exceptional influence in many fields of mathematics and science, and is ranked among history's most influential mathematicians. Quotes:
God does arithmetic.
Mathematicians stand on each other's shoulders.
The enchanting charms of this sublime science (mathematics) reveal only to those who have the courage to go deeply into it.

The problem of distinguishing prime numbers from composite numbers, and of resolving the latter into their prime factors, is known to be one of the most important and useful in arithmetic.

We must admit with humility that, while number is purely a product of our minds, space has a reality outside our minds, so that we cannot completely prescribe its properties a priori.

It is not knowledge, but the act of learning, not possession but the act of getting there, which grants the greatest enjoyment.

You know that I write slowly. This is chiefly because I am never satisfied until I have said as much as possible in a few words, and writing briefly takes far more time than writing at length.

- 7 February - 100th anniversary of the birth of **Godfrey Harold Hardy** (7 Feb 1877 – 1 Dec 1947, Cambridge, UK, aged 70.8), English mathematician, known for his achievements in number theory and mathematical analysis. In biology, he is known for the Hardy–Weinberg principle, a basic principle of population genetics (allele and genotype frequencies in a population will remain constant from generation to generation, in the absence of other evolutionary influences). Quote:

It is the mark of a truly intelligent person to be moved by statistics.

1978

- 4 March - 300th anniversary of the birth of Antonio Vivaldi (4 March 1678 – 28 July 1741, aged 63.3), great Italian (from Venezia) composer, virtuoso violinist, and teacher

- The author, 35, published his second review in the Mathematical Reviews of the American Mathematical Society, of an article published this year, regarding two generalizations of quasi-Kähler manifolds.

Chicago (1833): Chicago Water Works (down, 1869, was pumping station, survived fire in 1871, now base for the Lookingglass Theatre Company), Water Tower Place (right, 1976, 74 fl, 261 m), John Hancock Center (left up, 1969, 100 fl, 457 m with antenna).

1979

14 April – 350th anniversary of the birth of **Christaan Huygens** (14 April 1629 – 8 July 1695, aged 66.2, founder of mathematical physics, contributions in optics and mechanics, discovered Saturn's moon Titan, invention of the Huygenian eyepiece for the telescope, and invented the pendulum clock in 1656, which was a breakthrough in timekeeping, and became the most accurate timekeeper for almost 300 years)

- The author, 36, published his third review in the Mathematical Reviews of the American Mathematical Society, of an article published this year, regarding odd-dimensional extrinsic spheres in Kähler manifolds.

Rome (753 BC): the north side of Corte Suprema di Cassazione in Palazzo di Giustizia (1888 – 1911, 170 m by 155 m, covered with Travertine limestone), seen from Piazza Cavour.

Chapter 3. 1980 - 1989

1980

- 2600th anniversary of the birth of **Aesop** (c. 620 BC, Nesebar, Bulgaria – 564 BC, Delphi, Greece), Greek fabulist and storyteller, who wrote Aesop's Fables. Quotes:
Better be wise by the misfortunes of others than by your own.
In critical moments even the very powerful have need of the weakest.
It is thrifty to prepare today for the wants of tomorrow.
Injuries may be forgiven, but not forgotten.
It is easy to be brave from a safe distance.
United we stand, divided we fall.
No act of kindness, no matter how small, is ever wasted.
It is not only fine feathers that make fine birds.
A liar will not be believed, even when he speaks the truth.
We often give our enemies the means for our own destruction.
Slow and steady wins the race.
In union there is strength.
Gratitude is the sign of noble souls.

- 2550th anniversary of the birth of **Pythagoras** (570 BC – 495 BC, aged 75), great Greek mathematician. Pythagoras of Samos was born on the Samos Island, which is a Greek island in the eastern Aegean Sea, just 1.6 km from the coast of Asia Minor, where is Turkey, about 250 km East of Athens, and 350 km North-East of Crete. Pythagoras' quotes:
"Were it not for number and its nature, nothing that exists would be clear to anybody, either in itself, or in its relation to other things...You can observe the power of number exercising itself ... in all acts and the thoughts of men, in all handicrafts and music."

"As soon as laws are necessary for men, they are no longer fit for freedom."

Nosce te ipsum (Latin – Know thyself)

This Ancient Greek aphorism was inscribed in the pronaos (forecourt) of the Temple of Apollo at Delphi (120 km northwest of Athens, built about 150 years after the death of Pythagoras), and was translated in Latin by Cicero, about 450 years after the death of Pythagoras.

A thought is an idea in transit.

Above the cloud with its shadow is the star with its light. Above all things reverence thyself.

Choose rather to be strong of soul than strong of body.

Concern should drive us into action and not into a depression.

No man is free who cannot control himself.

Do not say a little in many words, but a great deal in a few.

Friends are as companions on a journey, who ought to aid each other to persevere in the road to a happier life.

It is better either to be silent, or to say things of more value than silence.

Rest satisfied with doing well, and leave others to talk of you as they will.

Silence is better than unmeaning words.

Strength of mind rests in sobriety; for this keeps your reason unclouded by passion.

The oldest, shortest words - "yes" and "no" - are those which require the most thought

- 15 October - 2050th anniversary of the birth of **Publius Vergilius Maro** (or Virgil, 15 Oct 70 BC – 21 Sep 19 BC, aged 50 years, 11 months and 6 days) in the farming village of Andes (now Virgilio), 6 km south of the city of Mantova (now Mantua, in Lombardia), 130 km southeast of Milano, in the Roman Republic province of Gallia Cisalpina, in northern Italy, to a wealthy equestrian farming family. Vergilius was raised on his family's farm, and the Italian countryside, with its people, which influenced him early on, was later echoed through his poetry. Vergilius died of fever at Brundisium harbor, Roman Empire (now Brindisi, Italia).

"Virgil's tomb" is found at the entrance of an ancient Roman tunnel ("grotta vecchia") in Piedigrotta, a district 3 km from the center of Napoli (Naples), near the Mergellina harbor, on the road heading north along the coast to Pozzuoli. It was a pilgrimage place for several centuries.

In Eclogue III, Vergilius writes in Latin:

Ab Iove principium (Let's start with Jupiter).

The Eclogues is the first of the three major works, pastorals, of Vergilius. He takes as his generic model the Greek Bucolica ("on care of cattle", poem in which shepherds converse). Literally it means to start from the most important person (because Jupiter was considered the leading of the Gods), or from the most important thing. This expression is used at the beginning of a debate, or an exposure, signaling that we'll start with the most important, or the principal assertion.

In the poem De rosis nascentibus, also called Idyllium de rosis, Vergilius writes:

Collige, virgo, rosas (gather, girl, the roses)

It encourages youth to enjoy life.

Other quotes:

Felix, qui potuit rerum cognoscere causas - Fortunate is he, who understood the causes of things.

Fervet opus - The work boils.

Facilis descensus Averno - The descent to hell is easy.

Famam extendere factis - To extend his fame by deeds.

Mens agitat molem – Mind drives matter.

Varium et mutabile semper femina – Woman is always a changeable and capricious thing.

O passi gravoria, dabit deus his quoque finem – Oh, suffering ones, God will grant an end to these things too.

Possunt quia posse videntur - They can because they think they can.

Adeo in teneris consuescere multum est - It is imperative to be well trained in early youth.

Ab uno disce omnes - From one example, learn all.

Ad utrumque paratus - Ready for both; prepared for either alternative.

Durate et vosmet rebus servate secundis - Carry on and preserve yourselves for better times.

Amor vincit omnia - Love conquers all.
Agnosco veteris vestigia flammae - I recognize the signs of the old flame.
Aeternum servans sub pectore vulnus - Nursing an everlasting wound within the breast.

- The author, 37, published his 4th and 5th reviews in the Mathematical Reviews of the American Mathematical Society, of an article published this year, regarding decompositions of the space of loops on a Lie group, and the geometrical relationship between a certain quadruple.

The east side of the Mausoleum (135-139) of Hadrian (76–138, Emperor 117-138, renamed Castel Sant'Angelo in 600).

1981

- 2450th anniversary of the birth of **Socrates** (469 BC – 399 BC, aged 70), classical Greek philosopher, one of the founders of Western philosophy, and the first moral philosopher. Quotes:

As for me, all I know is that I know nothing.

Be as you wish to seem.

Remember that there is nothing stable in human affairs; therefore avoid undue elation in prosperity, or undue depression in adversity.

It is not living that matters, but living rightly.

True wisdom comes to each of us when we comprehend how little we understand about life, ourselves, and the world around us.

Where there is reverence there is fear, but there is not reverence everywhere that there is fear, because fear presumably has a wider extension than reverence.

Worthless people live only to eat and drink; people of worth eat and drink only to live.

When the debate is over, slander becomes the tool of the loser.

Let him that would move the world, first move himself.

Beware the barrenness of a busy life.

Employ your time in improving yourself by other men's writings, so that you shall gain easily what others have labored hard for.

By all means marry. If you get a good wife, you'll be happy. If you get a bad one, you'll become a philosopher.

Education is the kindling of a flame, not the filling of a vessel.

I cannot teach anybody anything, I can only make them think.

- 20 January - **Ronald Wilson Reagan**, 69.9, (6 Feb 1911 – 5 June 2004, aged 93.3) was inaugurated as the 40th President of the United States, for 8 years, from 20 Jan 1981 to 20 Jan 1989. Prior to the presidency, he was a Hollywood actor and actors' trade union leader, before serving for 8 years as the 33rd Governor of California, from 1967 to 1975. Quotes:

Information is the oxygen of the modern age. It seeps through the walls topped by barbed wire, it wafts across the electrified borders.

It's true hard work never killed anybody, but I figure, why take the chance?

Man is not free unless government is limited.

Mr. Gorbachev, tear down this wall!

No mother would ever willingly sacrifice her sons for territorial gain, for economic advantage, for ideology.

No government ever voluntarily reduces itself in size. Government programs, once launched, never disappear. Actually, a government bureau is the nearest thing to eternal life we'll ever see on this earth!

No matter what time it is, wake me, even if it's in the middle of a Cabinet meeting.

- 15 March – 100 years ago, in 1881, the Romanian parliament raised the country to the status of a kingdom, and Carol (the German prince Charles of Hohenzollern-Sigmaringen (20 April 1839 – 10 Oct 1914, aged 75.5)) was crowned as king on 10 May 1881 (age 42), until 10 Oct 1914 (for 33.4 years). The motto of the Kingdom of Romania, while ruled by the Hohenzollern-Sigmaringen dynasty (1881–1947 (for 66 years)) was:

Nihil sine Deo (Latin) – **Nothing without God**

The motto is proudly displayed in the arms room of Peleş Castle in Sinaia.

- 13 June - 150th anniversary of the birth of **James Clerk Maxwell** (13 June 1831 – 5 Nov 1879, aged 48.4), Scottish mathematician in the field of mathematical physics. He formulated the classical theory of electromagnetic radiation, bringing together for the first time electricity, magnetism, and light. Quotes:

Ampère was the Newton of Electricity. (André-Marie Ampère (20 Jan 1775, Lyon, France - 10 June 1836, Marseille, France, aged 61.4) was a French mathematician and physicist, who was one of the founders of the classical electromagnetism, which he referred to as "electrodynamics". He is also the inventor of numerous applications, such as the solenoid and the electrical telegraph.)

1982

- 22 February – 250th anniversary of the birth of **George Washington** (February 22, 1732 – December 14, 1799, aged 67.8), an American soldier, farmer, land investor, politician, and statesman who served from 1789 to 1797 as the first President of the United States, and became known as the "Father of the United States". Quotes:

Happiness and moral duty are inseparably connected.

A slender acquaintance with the world must convince every man that actions, not words, are the true criterion of the attachment of friends.

Associate with men of good quality if you esteem your own reputation; for it is better to be alone than in bad company.

Discipline is the soul of an army. It makes small numbers formidable; procures success to the weak, and esteem to all.

Friendship is a plant of slow growth and must undergo and withstand the shocks of adversity before it is entitled to the appellation.

Government is not reason; it is not eloquent; it is force. Like fire, it is a dangerous servant and a fearful master.

I hope I shall possess firmness and virtue enough to maintain what I consider the most enviable of all titles, the character of an honest man.

If we desire to avoid insult, we must be able to repel it; if we desire to secure peace, one of the most powerful instruments of our rising prosperity, it must be known, that we are at all times ready for War.

Someday, following the example of the United States of America, there will be a United States of Europe.

The administration of justice is the firmest pillar of government.

The basis of our political system is the right of the people to make and to alter their constitutions of government.

The Constitution is the guide which I never will abandon.

Worry is the interest paid by those who borrow trouble.

USA, Boston, 20 June 2015, Boston Public Garden (1837), statue of George Washington (1732-1799), by Thomas Ball in 1869.

- 200 years ago, in 1782, the phrase
Novus ordo seclorum (Latin - **New order of the ages)**
appeared on the reverse of the Great Seal of the United States, first designed in 1782, and printed on the back of the United States one-dollar bill since 1935.

1983

- 28 February - 450th anniversary of the birth of **Michel Eyquem de Montaigne** (28 Feb 1533, Château de Montaigne – 13 Sep 1592, Château de Montaigne, aged 59.6), called Lord of Montaigne. He was one of the most significant French philosophers, known for popularizing the essay as a literary genre. His work Essais is well-known for its merging of casual anecdotes and autobiography, with intellectual insight. Quote:
I prefer the company of peasants, because they have not been educated sufficiently to reason incorrectly.

- 23 January - 200th anniversary of the birth of Marie-Henri Beyle, pen name **Stendhal** (23 Jan 1783, Grenoble, France – 23 March 1842, Paris, France, aged 59 years and 2 months), French writer, best known for the novels Le Rouge et le Noir and La Chartreuse de Parme. Quotes:
What is really beautiful must always be true.
A very small degree of hope is sufficient to cause the birth of love.
Life is too short, and the time we waste in yawning never can be regained.
Love has always been the most important business in my life, I should say the only one.
Mathematics allows for no hypocrisy and no vagueness.
One can acquire everything in solitude except character.
Only great minds can afford a simple style.
Pleasure is often spoiled by describing it.
The first qualification for a historian is to have no ability to invent.
The shepherd always tries to persuade the sheep that their interests and his own are the same.
To describe happiness is to diminish it.
In love, unlike most other passions, the recollection of what you have had and lost is always better than what you can hope for in the future.

- 7 May - 150ᵗʰ anniversary of the birth of **Johannes Brahms** (7 May 1833, Hamburg, Germany – 3 April 1897, Vienna, Austria, aged 63.9), German composer and pianist born in Hamburg, who spent much of his professional life in Vienna, Austria. Quote:

It is not hard to compose, but what is fabulously hard is to leave the superfluous notes under the table.

Japan, Kobe (201 AD, the 5ᵗʰ largest city in Japan, 30 km west of Osaka): a delightful Academy Bar, since 1922.

1984

- more than 1700 years ago, around 284, when there was persecution of Christians, and they were prohibited to possess the Scriptures, to meet on Sunday to celebrate the Eucharist, and to build premises for their assemblies, the Roman Christians responded:

Sine dominico non possumus (we cannot live without Sunday)

In the 19th and 20th centuries, **Non possumus** was the name given to the diplomatic policy of popes Pius IX, Leo XIII, Pius X, Benedict XV, Pius XI and Pius XII in their relations with foreign powers, especially after the capture of Rome, where the pontiff became the prisoner in the Vatican, and deliberately chose to limit his contacts with the outside world.

Rome (753 BC), Vatican (1929): Piazza di San Pietro (1656 – 1667, Bernini), with Moderno's façade (115 m wide, 46 m high) of the Basilica di San Pietro (1506 – 1626), and an Egyptian obelisk.

1985

- 1950th anniversary of the birth of **Marcus Fabius Quintilianus** (35, Calahorra, Hispania, Roman Empire – 100, Roma, Roman Empire, aged 65), Roman educator and rhetorician, extensively referred to in medieval schools of rhetoric and in Renaissance writing. Quotes:

Everything that has a beginning comes to an end.

It is the mother that the child first hears, and her words that he will first attempt to imitate.

Consequently, the student who is devoid of talent will derive no more profit from this work than unfertile soil from a treatise on agriculture.

For the mind is all the easier to teach before it is set.

We must form our minds by reading deep rather than wide.

It is much easier to try one's hand at many things than to concentrate one's powers on one thing.

We excuse our sloth under the pretext of difficulty.

A laugh costs too much when bought at the expense of virtue.

A laugh, if purchased at the expense of propriety, costs too much.

Mendacem memorem esse oportet - A liar needs a good memory.

- 31 March - 300th anniversary of the birth of **Johann Sebastian Bach** (31 March 1685 – 28 July 1750, aged 65.3), German composer and musician. He is known for instrumental compositions such as the Brandenburg Concertos and the Goldberg Variations, as well as for vocal music such as the St. Matthew Passion. He is regarded as one of the greatest composers of all time. Quotes:

I worked hard. Anyone who works as hard as I did can achieve the same results.

Music is an agreeable harmony for the honor of God and the permissible delights of the soul.

- 7 October - 100th anniversary of the birth of **Niels Bohr** (7 Oct 1885 – 18 Nov 1962, aged 77.1, Danish physicist who made important contributions to the theory of atomic structure and quantum theory, for which he received the Nobel Prize in Physics in 1922, at age 37. Bohr was also a philosopher and a promoter of scientific research.). Quotes:

Every great and deep difficulty bears in itself its own solution. It forces us to change our thinking in order to find it.

If quantum mechanics hasn't profoundly shocked you, you haven't understood it yet.

Technology has advanced more in the last thirty years than in the previous two thousands. The exponential increase in advancement will only continue.

The best weapon of a dictatorship is secrecy, but the best weapon of a democracy should be the weapon of openness.

There are some things so serious you have to laugh at them.

- 30 November - 150th anniversary of the birth of Samuel Langhorne Clemens, pen name **Mark Twain** (30 Nov 1835 – 21 April 1910, aged 74.4), American writer, humorist, entrepreneur, publisher, and lecturer. He is considered the father of the American literature. Quote:

In the first place, God made idiots. That was for practice. Then he made school boards.

- 8 December - 2050th anniversary of the birth of **Quintus Horatius Flaccus** (8 Dec 65 BC – 27 Nov 8 BC, Rome, Roman Empire, aged 56 years 11 months and 19 days (11 days before 57), in Venusia (City of Venus, now Venosa, elevation 415 m, in the province of Potenza, 130 km east of Napoli, 300 km southeast of Rome, 620 km southeast of Andes (now Virgilio)), a small town between the border regions of Apulia and Lucania (Basilicata, the Vulture area), in the Samnite (south of Italy) in the Roman Republic. Images of his childhood setting, and references to it, are found throughout his poems.

In his Ars Poetica (The Art of Poetry or On the Nature of Poetry), Horatius praises Homer that in his Iliad (written over 820

years before Horatius, around 890 BC) he stated that the Troy war started from the Greek Achilles hero's anger, and not
ab ovo (from the beginning),
that is not from the birth of Helen, who according to the legend was born from the Leda's egg. (Troy was a city, both factual and legendary, located in northwest Anatolia in what is now Turkey, southeast of the Dardanelles and beside Mount Ida. It is best known for being the setting of the Trojan War, described in the Greek Epic Cycle, and especially in the Iliad, one of the two epic poems attributed to Homer).

Expression used by Horatius in the Epistles, Book I, epistle IV, line 24:

Naturam expellas furca, tamen usque recurret (You may drive out Nature with a pitchfork, yet she still will hurry back).

From Horatius' Odes:

Nunc est bibendum, nunc pede libero pulsanda tellus (Now is the time to drink, now the time to dance footloose upon the earth)

From Horatius' Ode 1.11:

Carpe diem (Latin – Enjoy the day)

Ovidius, 21.3 years younger, was the first poet to use this aphorism. Then in 1648 Horatius' poem Carpe diem was translated in English by the English poet Robert Herrick (24 Aug 1591 – 15 Oct 1674, aged 83.1), and included in his book of poems Hesperides – then carpe diem became very famous.

Also from Horatius – meditation on the passing of time:

Ubi sunt? (Where are they?)

Carpe viam (Latin – Enjoy the road)

From Horatius' first book of Epistles:

Dimidium facti qui coepit habet: sapere aude, incipe (He who has begun is half done: dare to know, start)

Immanuel Kant (22 April 1724 – 12 February 1804, aged 79.8, German philosopher who is a central figure in modern philosophy) used "Sapere Aude" in his charge to readers to follow the program of intellectual self-liberation, the tool of which is Reason.

From Horatius' Epistles I:6, 67–68:

Si quid novisti rectius istis, candidus imperti; si nil, his utere mecum (If you can better these principles, tell me; if not, join me in following them)

A picture is a poem without words.

A word once uttered can never be recalled.

Adversity has the effect of eliciting talents, which in prosperous circumstances would have lain dormant.

Cease to inquire what the future has in store, and take as a gift whatever the day brings forth.

Choose a subject equal to your abilities; think carefully what your shoulders may refuse, and what they are capable of bearing.

He gains everyone's approval who mixes the pleasant with the useful.

He has the deed half done who has made a beginning.

He who postpones the hour of living is like the rustic who waits for the river to run out before he crosses.

In adversity remember to keep an even mind.

It is courage, courage, courage, that raises the blood of life to crimson splendor. Live bravely and present a brave front to adversity.

It is of no consequence of what parents a man is born, as long as he be a man of merit.

It is your business when the wall next door catches fire.

Labor diligently to increase your property.

Life grants nothing to us mortals without hard work.

Make a good use of the present.

Subdue your passion, or it will subdue you.

The disgrace of others often keeps tender minds from vice.

The foolish are like ripples on water, for whatsoever they do is quickly effaced; But the righteous are like carvings upon stone, for their smallest act is durable.

Whoever cultivates the golden mean avoids both the poverty of a hovel and the envy of a palace.

Why do you hasten to remove anything which hurts your eye, while if something affects your soul you postpone the cure until next year?

Why harass with eternal purposes a mind too weak to grasp them?

Words will not fail when the matter is well considered.

You must avoid sluggishness, that wicked siren.

Your own safety is at stake when your neighbor's wall is ablaze.

You traverse the world in search of happiness, which is within the reach of every man. A contented mind confers it on all.

Rome (753 BC): from Lungotevere Prati, the south-east side of the Mausoleum (right, 135-139) of Hadrian (76–138, Emperor 117-138, renamed Castel Sant'Angelo in 600).

1986

- 500 years ago, in 1486, Botticelli, 41, painted The Birth of Venus.

- The author, 43, published his 6th review in the Mathematical Reviews of the American Mathematical Society, of an article published this year, regarding the topology of the set of real m×n matrices of a certain rank.

Botticelli, 41, 1486, The Birth of Venus

1987

- 23 September - 2050th anniversary of the birth of Gaius Octavius, later **Augustus** (23 Sep 63 BC – 19 Aug 14, aged 75 years 10 month and 27 days (just 35 days before 76), being the first Roman emperor for 40 years and 7 months. Burial place: Mausoleum of Augustus in Rome. Quotes:

Festina lente - Make haste slowly.

Give me a safe commander, not a rash one.

I found Rome of clay; I leave it to you of marble.

Livia, ostri coniugii memor vive, ac vale - Livia, keep our marriage alive, and farewell.

Acta est fabula, plaudite! - The play is over, applaud! (The last words of the Roman Emperor Augustus)

- 700 years ago, in 1287, the popular academic song
Gaudeamus igitur (Let us rejoice)
appeared, on taking joy in student life.

The statue of Hadrian (76–138, Emperor 117-138) on the east side of his Mausoleum (135-139, renamed Castel Sant'Angelo in 600). Publius Aelius Traianus Hadrianus Augustus was the 14th Emperor of the Roman Empire, and had as predecessor Trajan (who named Hadrian emperor just before his death), and successor Antonius Pius. Hadrian built many temples in Athens. He adopted Antonius Pius (138-161) and asked him to adopt Marcus Aurelius (161-180).

1988

22 February - 200th anniversary of the birth of **Arthur Schopenhauer** (22 Feb 1788, Danzig, Prusia, 21 Sep 1860, Free City of Frankfurt, aged 72.6), German philosopher, best known for his 1818 (age 30) work The World as Will and Representation. Quotes:

A man can do what he wants. But he can't want what he wants.

Without books the development of civilization would have been impossible. They are the engines of change, windows on the world, "Lighthouses" as the poet said "erected in the sea of time." They are companions, teachers, magicians, bankers of the treasures of the mind. Books are humanity in print.

I've never known any trouble than an hour's reading didn't soften.

Compassion is the basis of morality.

To live alone is the fate of all great souls.

The two enemies of human happiness are pain and boredom.

A man can be himself only so long as he is alone.

Change alone is eternal, perpetual, immortal.

All truth passes through three stages. First, it is ridiculed. Second, it is violently opposed. Third, it is accepted as being self-evident.

Talent hits a target no one else can hit; Genius hits a target no one else can see.

Every man takes the limits of his own field of vision for the limits of the world.

Wealth is like sea-water; the more we drink, the thirstier we become; and the same is true of fame.

1989

- 30 August – 500th anniversary of the birth of Antonio Allegri da Correggio (30 Aug 1489, Correggio (now in Emilia-Romagna), Italia – 5 March 1534, Correggio, Italia, aged 44.6), Italian painter. Shortly before his death at only 44, in 1534, he finished his painting
Noli me tangere (Latin) - **Don't touch me /Touch me not**

Noli me Tangere by Antonio da Correggio, circa 1534, stored in the Museo del Prado.

This is the Latin version of words spoken, according to John 20:17, by Jesus to Mary Magdalene when she recognizes him after his resurrection. The biblical scene of Mary Magdalene's recognizing Jesus Christ after his resurrection became the subject of a continuous iconographic tradition in Christian art, from late antiquity to the present.

Chapter 4. 1990 - 1999

1990

- 2450th anniversary of the birth of **Hippocrates** (c. 460 BC, Island of Cos, Greece — c. 375 BC, Larissa, Thessaly, Greece, aged 85), Greek philosopher and physician, who wrote the Corpus Hippocraticum - he is the father of medicine. Quotes:

Walking is man's best medicine.
Cure sometimes, treat often, comfort always.
Everything in excess is opposed to nature.
Extreme remedies are very appropriate for extreme diseases.
Healing is a matter of time, but it is sometimes also a matter of opportunity.
If we could give every person the right amount of nourishment and exercise, not too little and not too much, we would have found the safest way to health.
Keep a watch also on the faults of the patients, which often make them lie about the taking of things prescribed.
Let food be thy medicine and medicine be thy food.
Life is short, the art long.
Wherever the art of medicine is loved, there is also a love of humanity.
It is more important to know what sort of person has a disease, than to know what sort of disease a person has.
There are in fact two things, science and opinion; the former begets knowledge, the latter ignorance.
Natural forces within us are the true healers of disease.
Make a habit of two things: to help; or at least to do no harm.

- 2450th anniversary of the birth of **Democritus** (c. 460 BC, Abdera, Thrace, Greece – c 370 BC, Greece, aged 90) was an

Ancient Greek philosopher, who formulated an atomic theory of the universe, and emphasized the value of cheerfulness. Quotes:

By desiring little, a poor man makes himself rich.

Everything existing in the universe is the fruit of chance and necessity.

Good means not merely not to do wrong, but rather not to desire to do wrong.

Happiness resides not in possessions, and not in gold, happiness dwells in the soul.

I would rather discover one scientific fact than gain the kingdom of Persia.

It is greed to do all the talking but not to want to listen at all.

Nothing exists except atoms and empty space; everything else is opinion.

- 2450th anniversary of the birth of **Thucydides** (460 BC, Alimos, Greece – 395 BC, Athens, Greece, aged 65), Athenian historian, author and general. His History of the Peloponnesian War recounts the fifth-century BC war, for nearly 30 years, between Sparta and Athens until the year 411 BC, when he was 49. Quotes:

Ignorance is bold and knowledge reserved.

Be convinced that to be happy means to be free, and that to be free means to be brave. Therefore, do not take lightly the perils of war.

History is Philosophy teaching by examples.

Justice will not come to Athens until those who are not injured are as indignant as those who are injured.

The bravest are surely those who have the clearest vision of what is before them, glory and danger alike, and yet, notwithstanding, go out to meet it.

The secret to happiness is freedom... And the secret to freedom is courage.

Few things are brought to a successful issue by impetuous desire, but most by calm and prudent forethought.

- 1600th anniversary of the birth of **Publius Flavius Vegetius Renatus** (390 – 450, aged 60), usually called Vegetius, who was a Roman military expert who wrote the single most influential military book (in four volumes) De re militari or Epitoma rei militaris (Latin "Concerning Military Matters"). Quotes:

Si vis pacem, para bellum (Latin - If you want peace, prepare for war)

Also: **Igitur qui desiderat pacem, praeparet bellum** (Therefore who desires peace, prepares for war)

Few men are born brave. Many become so through training and force of discipline.

The courage of a soldier is heightened by his knowledge of his profession.

Valor is superior to number.

The National Museum of the United States Air Force (1923, Dayton, Ohio, the world's largest and oldest military aviation museum): Boeing B-29 Superfortress "Bockscar" (1942-1946).

1991

- 2500 years ago, in 509 BC, the last King of Rome was expelled, and the Roman Republic was founded (traditional date). The official name of the Roman Republic was
 Senatus Populusque Romanus (SPQR) (The Senate and the People of Rome**).**
"SPQR" was carried on battle standards by the Roman legions. In addition to being an ancient Roman motto, it remains the motto of the modern city of Rome.

- The author, 48, published his 7th review in the Mathematical Reviews of the American Mathematical Society, of an article published this year, regarding multivariate Sturm theory.

Rome (753 BC): the east side of Pons Aelius (Bridge of Hadrian, 134 AD, 18 m, 5 spans, renamed Ponte Sant'Angelo in 600), south of Mausoleum (135-139) of Hadrian (76–138, Emperor 117-138, renamed Castel Sant'Angelo in 600), with 10 statues of angels.

1992

29 February – 200th anniversary of the birth of **Gioachino Rossini** (29 February 1792 – 13 November 1868, aged 76.7, Italian composer who wrote 39 operas, as well as some sacred music, songs, chamber music, and piano pieces; he was a precocious composer of operas, and he made his debut at age 18). Quotes:

Give me a laundry-list and I'll set it to music.

Answer them [critics] with silence and indifference. It works better, I assure you, than anger and argument.

Thou knowest, O Lord, as well as I, that really I am only a composer of opera buffa.

- The author, 49, published his 8th and 9th reviews in the Mathematical Reviews of the American Mathematical Society, of a book (which was a 118 pages dissertation at Technische Universiteit Eindhoven) published this year, regarding algebraic-geometric codes and their decoding algorithm, and of an article published this year, regarding a new authentication system based on the generalized affine planes.

Chicago (1833, 2.7 million): Whitehall Hotel (1927, red, right) on E. Delaware Pl., Fourth Presbyterian Church (left down, 1871).

1993

- 4 January – 350th anniversary of the birth of Sir **Isaac Newton** (4 Jan 1643 – 31 March 1727, aged 84.2), great English mathematician, astronomer, theologian, author and physicist. Quote:

Natura valde simplex est et sibi consona (Latin) - **Nature is exceedingly simple and harmonious with itself.**

I do not know what I may appear to the world; but to myself I seem to have been only like a boy playing on the seashore, and diverting myself now and then finding a smoother pebble or a prettier shell than ordinary, whilst the great ocean of truth lay all undiscovered before me.

If I have seen further than others, it is by standing upon the shoulders of giants.

Men build too many walls and not enough bridges.

Tact is the art of making a point without making an enemy.

UK, Cambridge, a bas-relief on the eastern wall of the western building of the Old Court (1451) of Queens' College (1448),

University of Cambridge, 60 m east of the Mathematical Bridge (1749).

- 13 April - 250th anniversary of the birth of **Thomas Jefferson** (13 April 1743, Shadwell, VA, English America – 4 July 1826, Monticello, VA, USA, aged 83.2), American Founding Father, who was the principal author of the Declaration of Independence, and later served as the third President of the United States from 1801 to 1809. Previously, he had been elected the second Vice President of the United States, serving under John Adams from 1797 to 1801. Quotes:
    When governments fear the people there is liberty. When the people fear the government there is tyranny.
    Information is the currency of democracy.
    A Bill of Rights is what the people are entitled to against every government, and what no just government should refuse, or rest on inference.
    A wise and frugal Government, which shall restrain men from injuring one another, which shall leave them otherwise free to regulate their own pursuits of industry and improvement, and shall not take from the mouth of labor the bread it has earned. This is the sum of good government, and this is necessary to close the circle of our felicities.
    All tyranny needs to gain a foothold is for people of good conscience to remain silent.
    An association of men who will not quarrel with one another is a thing which has never yet existed, from the greatest confederacy of nations down to a town meeting or a vestry.
    An enemy generally says and believes what he wishes.
    Books constitute capital. A library book lasts as long as a house, for hundreds of years. It is not, then, an article of mere consumption but fairly of capital, and often in the case of professional men, setting out in life, it is their only capital.
    When angry, count to ten before you speak. If very angry, count to one hundred.
    Whenever you do a thing, act as if the entire world were watching.

- The author, 50, published his 10th, 11th and 12th reviews in the Mathematical Reviews of the American Mathematical Society, of three articles published this year, regarding a geometrical approach to curvature continuous joints of rational curves, algebraically rectifiable parametric curves, and la détermination des points isolés et de la dimension d'une variété algébrique peut se faire en temps polynomial (which is a chapter in the book Computational algebraic geometry and commutative algebra (Cortona, 1991), 216–256).

Rome (753 BC), Vatican City State (1929): interior of the Basilica Papale di San Pietro (1506 – 1626,), with a chapel on the north aisle with a painting by Pietro da Cortona (1596 – 1669).

1994

- 3 January - 2100th anniversary of the birth of **Marcus Tullius Cicero** (3 Jan 106 BC – 7 Dec 43 BC, aged 63.9, Roman statesman, orator and philosopher, who served as consul in the year 63 BC). Cicero's quotes:

Gratitude is not only the greatest of virtues, but the parent of all the others.

Adhibenda est in iocando moderatio - One should employ restraint in his jests.

Damnant quodnon intelligunt - They condemn what they do not understand

Dum spiro, spero - While there's life, there's hope.

The more laws, the less justice.

Before beginning, plan carefully.

Brevity is a great charm of eloquence.

To live is to think.

A home without books is a body without soul.

Silence is one of the great arts of conversation.

Cultivation to the mind is as necessary as food to the body.

Thou shouldst eat to live; not live to eat

What gift has providence bestowed on man that is so dear to him as his children?

Nature has planted in our minds an insatiable longing to see the truth

From Cicero's De Legibus, book III, part III, sub. VIII:

Salus populi suprema lex esto - (Latin - The welfare of the people is to be the highest law)

It has been quoted by John Locke (29 Aug 1632 – 28 Oct 1704, aged 72.1) in his Second Treatise, on Civil Government, to describe the proper organization of government.

- 21 November – 300th anniversary of the birth of François-Marie Arouet (21 November 1694 – 30 May 1778, aged 83.5), known by his nom de plume **Voltaire**, a French writer, historian and philosopher famous for his wit, and his advocacy of freedom of religion, freedom of speech, and separation of church and state. Voltaire was a versatile and prolific writer, producing works in almost every literary form, including plays, poems, novels, essays, and historical and scientific works. He wrote more than 20,000 letters, and more than 2,000 books and pamphlets. Quote:

A human being is not attaining his full heights until he is educated.

Men who are occupied in the restoration of health to other men, by the joint exertion of skill and humanity, are above all the great of the Earth. They even partake of divinity, since to preserve and renew is almost as noble as to create.

Work saves us from three great evils: boredom, vice and need.

A multitude of laws in a country is like a great number of physicians, a sign of weakness and malady.

It is the characteristic of the most stringent censorships that they give credibility to the opinions they attack.

It is dangerous to be right when the government is wrong.

Perfection is attained by slow degrees; it requires the hand of time.

Let us read and let us dance - two amusements that will never do any harm to the world.

The way to become boring is to say everything.

Common sense is not so common.

We must cultivate our own garden. When man was put in the Garden of Eden he was put there so that he should work, which proves that man was not born to rest.

- The author, 51, published his 13th and 14th reviews in the Mathematical Reviews of the American Mathematical Society, of two articles published this year, regarding surface intersection using parallelism, and on the main conjecture of geometric MDS codes.

1995

– 600th anniversary of the birth of Beato Angelico (Fra Angelico, born Guido di Pietro; c. 1395 – February 18, 1455, aged c. 59.5), Italian painter, with his famous painting "Annunciation" (c. 1430, when he was 35) in Diocesan Museum in Cortona.

- 100 years ago, in 1895, Wilhelm Röntgen identifies x-rays.

- The author, 52, published his 15th and 16th reviews in the Mathematical Reviews of the American Mathematical Society, of two articles published this year, regarding discrepancy operators and numerical integration on compact groups, and on algorithmic parametrization methods in algebraic geometry.

Italy, 8 Sep 1977, Sophia Dediu (34) at Cortona (20 km southeast of Arezzo (circa 1500 BC, 343 km^2, elevation 494 m, population 23,000)), the southwest façade and entrance of Il Palazzone di Cortona (1521-1527, 2 km southeast of Cortona).

1996

- 2250th anniversary of the birth of **Titus Maccius Plautus** (c. 254 BC – c 184 BC, aged c. 70), better known simply as Plautus (actually a nickname meaning 'flatfoot'), who was the best-known Roman playwright. His comedies are the earliest Latin literary works to have survived in their entirety, and are at a very high rank among the comic writers of the world. Plautus' quote:
Dictum sapienti sat est (Enough has been said for the wise)
Indicates that something can be understood without any need for explanation, if the listener has enough wisdom or common sense.

- 2000th anniversary of the birth of **Lucius Annaeus Seneca** (4 BC – 12 April 65 AD, aged 68), Roman Stoic philosopher, statesman and dramatist. Quotes:
Man is something sacred for man.
Luck is what happens when preparation meets opportunity.
One of the most beautiful qualities of true friendship is to understand and to be understood.
Wherever there is a human being, there is an opportunity for a kindness.
To govern is to serve, not to rule.
Errare humanum est, perseverare diabolicum (To err is human, to persist – diabolical)
Si vis amari ama (Latin - If you want to be loved, love)
Non est ad astra mollis e terris via - There is no easy way from the Earth to the stars.
Homines dum docent discunt - Men learn while they teach.

- 31 March – 400th anniversary of the birth of **René Descartes** (Renatus Cartesius; adjectival form: "Cartesian"; 31 March 1596 – 11 February 1650, aged 53.9), French mathematician, philosopher, and scientist. He is the father of analytical geometry and of modern Western philosophy. Quotes:
A state is better governed which has few laws, and those laws strictly observed.

An optimist may see a light where there is none, but why must the pessimist always run to blow it out?

Common sense is the most fairly distributed thing in the world, for each one thinks he is so well-endowed with it, that, even those who are hardest to satisfy in all other matters, are not in the habit of desiring more of it, than they already have.

Nothing is more fairly distributed than common sense: no one thinks he needs more of it than he already has.

Divide each difficulty into as many parts as is feasible and necessary to resolve it.

Except our own thoughts, there is nothing absolutely in our power.

I am indeed amazed when I consider how weak my mind is, and how prone to error.

I hope that posterity will judge me kindly, not only as to the things which I have explained, but also to those which I have intentionally omitted so as to leave to others the pleasure of discovery.

I think; therefore I exist.

Illusory joy is often worth more than genuine sorrow.

It is not enough to have a good mind; the main thing is to use it well.

It is only prudent never to place complete confidence in that by which we have even once been deceived.

One cannot conceive anything so strange and so implausible that it has not already been said by one philosopher or another.

Perfect numbers, like perfect men, are very rare.

The first precept was never to accept a thing as true until I knew it as such without a single doubt.

The reading of all good books is like a conversation with the finest minds of past centuries.

The two operations of our understanding, intuition and deduction, on which alone, we have said, we must rely in the acquisition of knowledge.

When it is not in our power to follow what is true, we ought to follow what is most probable.

- The author, 53, published his 17th to 22nd reviews in the Mathematical Reviews of the American Mathematical Society, of 6 articles published this year, regarding an SQP algorithm for finely discretized continuous minimax problems and other minimax problems with many objective functions, maximum entropy methods for constrained optimization and minimax problems, geometric continuity between adjacent Bézier patches and their constructions, the Gaussian and mean curvature criteria for curvature continuity between surfaces, potential applications of Weingarten surfaces in CAGD. I. Weingarten surfaces and surface shape investigation, and a Darboux's problem for sequences of polygons.

Venezia: Libreria (left), San Theodore Column, Palazzo Ducale, Lion of Venice Column (center) on Riva degli Schiavoni street.

1997

- 11 February - 150th anniversary of the birth of **Thomas Alva Edison** (February 11, 1847 – October 18, 1931, aged 84.6), American inventor and businessman, who is America's greatest inventor. He developed many devices that greatly influenced life around the world, including the phonograph, the motion picture camera, and the practical electric light bulb. Quotes:

Anything that won't sell, I don't want to invent. Its sale is proof of utility, and utility is success.

Be courageous. I have seen many depressions in business. Always America has emerged from these stronger and more prosperous. Be brave as your fathers before you. Have faith! Go forward!

Being busy does not always mean real work. The object of all work is production or accomplishment, and to either of these ends there must be forethought, system, planning, intelligence, and honest purpose, as well as perspiration. Seeming to do is not doing.

Discontent is the first necessity of progress.

Everything comes to him who hustles while he waits.

Hell, there are no rules here - we're trying to accomplish something.

I am proud of the fact that I never invented weapons to kill.

I find my greatest pleasure, and so my reward, in the work that precedes what the world calls success.

I have friends in overalls whose friendship I would not swap for the favor of the kings of the world.

I have not failed. I've just found 10,000 ways that won't work.

I know this world is ruled by infinite intelligence. Everything that surrounds us- everything that exists - proves that there are infinite laws behind it. There can be no denying this fact. It is mathematical in its precision.

I never did a day's work in my life. It was all fun.

I never did anything by accident, nor did any of my inventions come by accident; they came by work.

I start where the last man left off.

If we did all the things we are capable of, we would literally astound ourselves.

It is astonishing what an effort it seems to be for many people to put their brains definitely and systematically to work.

Just because something doesn't do what you planned it to do, doesn't mean it's useless.

Maturity is often more absurd than youth, and very frequently is most unjust to youth.

Nearly every man who develops an idea works it up to the point where it looks impossible, and then he gets discouraged. That's not the place to become discouraged.

Non-violence leads to the highest ethics, which is the goal of all evolution.

Opportunity is missed by most people because it is dressed in overalls and looks like work.

Our greatest weakness lies in giving up. The most certain way to succeed is always to try just one more time.

The best thinking has been done in solitude. The worst has been done in turmoil.

The chief function of the body is to carry the brain around.

The three great essentials to achieve anything worthwhile are: Hard work, Stick-to-itiveness, and Common sense.

The value of an idea lies in the using of it.

There is far more opportunity than there is ability.

There is no expedient to which a man will not go to avoid the labor of thinking.

There is no substitute for hard work.

There will one day spring from the brain of science a machine or force so fearful in its potentialities, so absolutely terrifying, that even man, the fighter, who will dare torture and death in order to inflict torture and death, will be appalled, and so abandon war forever.

There's a way to do it better - find it.

To invent, you need a good imagination and a pile of junk.

Waste is worse than loss. The time is coming when every person who lays claim to ability will keep the question of waste before him constantly. The scope of thrift is limitless.

We don't know a millionth of one percent about anything.

What a man's mind can create, man's character can control.

What you are will show in what you do.

When I have fully decided that a result is worth getting, I go ahead of it, and make trial after trial until it comes.

Your worth consists in what you are and not in what you have.

- 21 April - 2750 years ago, in 753 BC, Rome was founded (traditional), by Romulus, the founder of the fortress. For many centuries after that, the Romans counted the years from this date, using the Latin expression

Ab urbe condita (AUC) or **Urbis conditae (U.C.)** (From the foundation of the city)

The Roman calendar was counted Ab urbe condita, and it continued to be in use for over 1275 years, until the Anno Domini calendar was introduced in AD 525 = 1278 AUC, therefore 19 BC = 734 AUC, and 2019 = 2772 AUC. The Roman's History books by Titus Livius Patavinus (59 BC, Padova, Roman Republic – 17 AD, Padova, Roman Empire, aged 76, Roman historian) are called Ab urbe condita libri.

- The author, 54, published his 23rd to 26th reviews in the Mathematical Reviews of the American Mathematical Society, of 4 articles published this year, regarding piecewise rational approximations of real algebraic curves, rational parametrizations of algebraic curves using a canonical divisor. Parametric algebraic curves and applications, polynomial-time computation of the dimensions of components of algebraic varieties in zero-characteristic. Algorithms for algebra, and stable approximations of a minimal surface problem with variational inequalities.

Rome (753 BC): la Chiesa Parrochiale del Sacro Cuore del Suffragio (1894 – 1917, by Giuseppe Gualandi) on Lungotevere Prati, 50 m east of the Corte Suprema di Cassazione in Palazzo di Giustizia (1888 – 1911).

1998

- January - 450th anniversary of the birth of **Giordano Bruno** (January 1548, Nola, near Napoli, Italia – 17 February 1600, Campo de'Fiori, Roma, Italia, aged 52.1), Italian Dominican friar (his baptismal name was Filippo, but he took the name Giordano, by which he is always known, on entering the Dominican order), philosopher, mathematician, poet, astronomer and cosmological theorist, who extended the Copernican model - every exoplanet confirms not the cosmology of Kepler, but of Giordano Bruno. Quotes:

It is proof of a base and low mind for one to wish to think with the masses or majority, merely because the majority is the majority. Truth does not change because it is, or is not, believed by a majority of the people.

It may be you fear more to deliver judgment upon me than I fear judgment.

Time takes all and gives all.

Time is the father of truth, its mother is our mind.

- over 2500 years ago, the Ancient Greeks used the word
parasitos
to describe someone who ate at your table, but never invited you back. Now, in general, on this planet, it is estimated that less than 60% of the working-able people actually work something useful, the rest, over 40% of the working-able people, are parasites. This is called the 60/40 rule, and the general objective is to change it to 90/10 or better.

1999

- 2550th anniversary of the birth of **Confucius** (551 BC – 479 BC, aged 72), a Chinese teacher, editor, politician, and philosopher of the Spring and Autumn period of Chinese history. Confucianism underlines personal and governmental morality, correctness of social relationships, justice and sincerity. Quotes:

Do not impose on others what you yourself do not desire.

What you do not want done to yourself, do not do to others.

Wisdom, compassion, and courage are the three universally recognized moral qualities of men.

Without feelings of respect, what is there to distinguish men from beasts?

You cannot open a book without learning something.

Success depends upon previous preparation, and without such preparation there is sure to be failure.

The cautious seldom err.

The superior man acts before he speaks, and afterwards speaks according to his action.

To be wronged is nothing, unless you continue to remember it.

When a country is governed well, poverty and mean condition are things to be ashamed of. When a country is governed poorly, riches and honor are things to be ashamed of.

The more man meditates upon good thoughts, the better will be his world and the world at large.

The strength of a nation derives from the integrity of the home.

The superior man is distressed by the limitations of his ability; he is not distressed by the fact that men do not recognize the ability that he has.

The superior man is modest in his speech, but exceeds in his actions.

The superior man makes the difficulty, to be overcome, his first interest; success only comes later.

The will to win, the desire to succeed, the urge to reach your full potential... these are the keys that will unlock the door to personal excellence.

When anger rises, think of the consequences.

When it is obvious that the goals cannot be reached, don't adjust the goals, adjust the action steps.

When we see persons of worth, we should think of equaling them.

I hear and I forget. I see and I remember. I do and I understand.

He who learns but does not think, is lost! He who thinks but does not learn, is in great danger.

To practice five things under all circumstances constitutes perfect virtue; these five are gravity, generosity of soul, sincerity, earnestness, and kindness.

The superior man thinks always of virtue; the common man thinks of comfort.

The superior man understands what is right; the inferior man understands what will sell.

Better a diamond with a flaw than a pebble without.

By three methods we may learn wisdom: First, by reflection, which is noblest; Second, by imitation, which is easiest; and third by experience, which is the bitterest.

Choose a job you love, and you will never have to work a day in your life.

A superior man is modest in his speech, but exceeds in his actions.

Ability will never catch up with the demand for it.

An oppressive government is more to be feared than a tiger.

Study the past if you would divine the future.

With coarse rice to eat, with water to drink, and my bent arm for a pillow -- I have still joy in the midst of all these things.

The perfecting of one's self is the fundamental base of all progress and all moral development.

The real fault is to have faults and not amend them.

He acts before he speaks, and afterwards speaks according to his actions.

The mind of the superior man is conversant with virtue; the mind of the base man is conversant with gain.

28 August - 250th anniversary of the birth of **Johann Wolfgang von Goethe** (28 August 1749 – 22 March 1832, aged 82.6), German writer and statesman. His works include four novels; epic and lyric poetry; prose and verse dramas; memoirs; an autobiography; literary and aesthetic criticism; and treatises on botany, anatomy, and color. Quotes:

A man who is ignorant of foreign languages is also ignorant of his own language.

All intelligent thoughts have already been thought; what is necessary is only to try to think them again.

A creation of importance can only be produced when its author isolates himself, it is a child of solitude.

A noble person attracts noble people, and knows how to hold on to them.

All things are only transitory.

Beauty is everywhere a welcome guest.

What is not started today is never finished tomorrow.

Which government is the best? The one that teaches us to govern ourselves.

Wisdom is found only in truth.

- 20 May - 200th anniversary of the birth of **Honoré de Balzac** (20 May 1799 – 18 August 1850, aged 51.2, French novelist and playwright). Quotes:

A good husband is never the first to go to sleep at night or the last to awake in the morning.

A mother who is really a mother is never free.

An unfulfilled vocation drains the color from a man's entire existence.

It is easy to sit down and take notice, what is difficult is getting up and taking action.

Laws are spider webs through which the big flies pass and the little ones get caught.

Love is the poetry of the senses.

Power is action; the electoral principle is discussion. No political action is possible when discussion is permanently established.

Solitude is fine, but you need someone to tell you that solitude is fine.

The duration of passion is proportionate with the original resistance of the woman.

The heart of a mother is a deep abyss at the bottom of which you will always find forgiveness.

The more one judges, the less one loves.

The motto of chivalry is also the motto of wisdom; to serve all, but love only one.

There is no such thing as a great talent without great will power.

True love is eternal, infinite, and always like itself. It is equal and pure, without violent demonstrations: it is seen with white hairs and is always young in the heart.

- about 600 years ago, in 1399, there were cheerful songs, which included the Latin expressions:

Vitam mutaveris in meliores actus (Change your life for the better)

Festinamus errare (Let us refrain from erring)

- The author, 56, published his 27th to 33rd reviews in the Mathematical Reviews of the American Mathematical Society, of 7 articles published this year, regarding the geometry of algorithms with orthogonality constraints, convexity preserving interpolation, codes for spread spectrum applications generated using chaotic dynamical systems, a class of nonmonotone conjugate gradient methods for unconstrained optimization, differential geometry of intersection curves of two surfaces, on the minimal length curve that densifies the square, and emerging tools for experimental mathematics.

Chicago (1833): Fourth Presbyterian Church (right center, 1871), Elysées Condominiums (center-right, 1972, 56 floors, 161 m), Loyola University of Chicago (red center down, 1870, 1927 this building), Park Tower (center-left, 2000, 67 floors, 257 m).

Chapter 5. 2000 - 2009

2000

- 2850th anniversary of the birth of **Homer** (c. 850 BC – c. 780 BC, aged c. 70), ancient Greek epic poet of the Odyssey and Iliad. Quotes:

For rarely are sons similar to their fathers: most are worse, and a few are better than their fathers.

In youth and beauty, wisdom is but rare!

There is nothing nobler or more admirable than when a man and a woman, who see eye to eye, keep house as man and wife, confounding their enemies, and delighting their friends.

- 2100th anniversary of the birth of **Gaius Julius Caesar** (100 BC- 44 BC, aged 56), Roman general, statesman and writer. Quotes:

Ab imo pectore - From the bottom of the chest (heart).

Fere libenter homines id quod volunt credunt - Men willingly believe, what they want to believe.

Alea iacta est - The die is cast.

Veni vidi vici - I came, I saw, I conquered.

What we wish, we readily believe, and what we ourselves think, we imagine others think also.

- 1950th anniversary of the birth of **Epictetus** (50, Hierapolis, Phrygia, Roman Empire – 130, Nicopolis, Greece, Roman Empire, aged 80), Greek speaking (epiktetos in Greek means "acquired") Stoic philosopher. He lived in Rome, then in Nicopolis, in northwestern Greece. His teachings were written down and published by his pupil Arrian in his Discourses and Enchiridion (the handbook).

Only the educated are free.

Control thy passions lest they take vengeance on thee.

Difficulties are things that show a person what they are.
Freedom is not procured by a full enjoyment of what is desired, but by controlling the desire.
No man is free who is not master of himself.
It's not what happens to you, but how you react to it that matters.
We have two ears and one mouth so that we can listen twice as much as we speak.
He is a wise man who does not grieve for the things which he has not, but rejoices for those which he has.

- 500 years ago, in 1500, Leonardo da Vinci, 48, (1452 – 1519, aged 67, Italian painter, sculptor, architect, mathematician, and inventor) used the Latin expression
Salvator Mundi (Savior of the World)
as the title for his famous painting (which was sold, after 517 years, for a world record $450.3 M at a Christie's auction in New York, on 15 November 2017, the highest price ever paid for a work of art). Quotes:
A well-spent day brings happy sleep.
Art is never finished, only abandoned.
Learning never exhausts the mind.
Nothing strengthens authority so much as silence.

- 8 February - 300th anniversary of the birth of **Daniel Bernoulli** (8 February1700 – 17 March 1782, aged 82.1), Swiss mathematician and physicist, one of the many prominent mathematicians in the Bernoulli family. He is remembered for his applications of mathematics to mechanics, especially fluid mechanics, and for his work in probability and statistics. His name is commemorated in the Bernoulli's principle, an example of the conservation of energy, which describes the mathematics of the mechanism underlying the operation of two important technologies of the 20th century: the carburetor and the airplane wing. Quotes:
There is no philosophy which is not founded upon knowledge of the phenomena, but to get any profit from this knowledge it is absolutely necessary to be a mathematician.
Nature always tends to act in the simplest way.

All birds need to fly are the right-shaped wings, the right pressure and the right angle.

- The author, 57, published his 34th to 38th reviews in the Mathematical Reviews of the American Mathematical Society, of 5 articles published this year, regarding when does a dynamic programming formulation guarantee the existence of a fully polynomial time approximation scheme (FPTAS)?, the projective Noether Maple package: computing the dimension of a projective variety, blind identification of an autoregressive system using a nonlinear dynamical approach, (t,n) threshold untraceable signatures, and the warm-up algorithm: a Lagrangian construction of length restricted Huffman codes.

Japan, Kobe (201 AD, the 5th largest city in Japan, 30 km west of Osaka): inside the Sogo store, located in Hanshin Railway Sannomiya Station, on Flower Road, the customers can see beautiful decorations for Christmas 2008 in Kobe.

2001

- 29 September - 100th anniversary of the birth of **Enrico Fermi** (29 Sep 1901 – 28 Nov 1954, aged 53.1), who was an Italian and naturalized-American physicist, and the creator of the world's first nuclear reactor, the Chicago Pile-1. Fermi held several patents related to the use of nuclear power, and was awarded, at age 37, the 1938 Nobel Prize in Physics for his work on induced radioactivity by neutron bombardment, and for the discovery of transuranium elements. He made significant contributions to the development of statistical mechanics, quantum theory, and nuclear and particle physics. Quotes:

Before I came here, I was confused about this subject. Having listened to your lecture I am still confused. But on a higher level.

If I could remember the names of all these particles, I'd be a botanist.

The fundamental point in fabricating a chain reacting machine is of course to see to it that each fission produces a certain number of neutrons, and some of these neutrons will again produce fission.

- The author, 58, published his 39th to 44th reviews in the Mathematical Reviews of the American Mathematical Society, of 6 articles published this year, regarding dynamic programming and the graphical representation of error-correcting codes, correlation theorems in cryptanalysis, how good can polynomial interpolation on the sphere be?, employ a data compression scheme to speed up the computations on elliptic curves, comparison of formulations and solution methods for image restoration problems, and moderate-density burst error-locating linear codes.

Chicago (1833): 900 North Michigan (1989, 66 fl, 265 m). Fourth Presbyterian Church (center-left down, 1871).

2002

– 26 February – 200th anniversary of the birth of **Victor Hugo** (26 February 1802 – 22 May 1885, aged 83.2), French poet, novelist, and dramatist, considered to be one of the greatest and best-known French writers. Quote:

Intelligence without ambition is a bird without wings.

He, who opens a school door, closes a prison.

Life is the flower for which love is the honey.

A library implies an act of faith.

A man is not idle because he is absorbed in thought. There is a visible labor and there is an invisible labor.

A mother's arms are made of tenderness, and children sleep soundly in them.

All the forces in the world are not so powerful as an idea whose time has come.

To rise from error to truth is rare and beautiful.

What a grand thing, to be loved! What a grander thing still, to love!

When dictatorship is a fact, revolution becomes a right.

When grace is joined with wrinkles, it is adorable. There is an unspeakable start in happy old age.

- The author, 59, published his 45th to 50th reviews in the Mathematical Reviews of the American Mathematical Society, of 5 articles and one book published this year, regarding inapproximability of finding maximum hidden sets on polygons and terrains, phase retrieval, error reduction algorithm, and Fienup variants: a view from convex optimization, bounds on packings of spheres in the Grassmann manifold, (the next is a book with 324 pages) introduction to cryptography. Principles and applications, Euler's elastica and curvature-based inpainting, and algorithm 820: a flexible implementation of matching pusuit for Gabor functions on the interval.

Italy, Rome (753 BC, one of the oldest continuously occupied cities in Europe, called Roma Aeterna (The Eternal City) and Caput Mundi (Capital of the World)), in Villa Borghese (1630), a monument (1905, by Lucien Pallez, donated by the French Government) to Victor Hugo (1802 – 1885, the greatest French writer (Hernani (1830, inspired opera Ernani (1844) by Giuseppe Verdi (1813-1901)), Notre-Dame de Paris (1831), Le roi s'amuse (1832, inspired opera Rigoletto (1851) by Giuseppe Verdi)), Les Misérables (1862), Les Contemplations, La Légendre des siècles)).

2003

- 400 years ago, in 1603, Accademia Nazionale dei Lincei was founded in Rome.

- The author, 60, published his 51st to 55th reviews in the Mathematical Reviews of the American Mathematical Society, of 5 articles and one book published this year, regarding the identification of sets of points in the square lattice, curve interpolation based on Catmull-Clark subdivision scheme, (the next is a book with 301 pages) Space-time block coding for wireless communications, a block-iterative surrogate constraint splitting method for quadratic signal recovery, enhancing Levin's method for computing quadric-surface intersections, and overview of approximate implicitization. Chapter from Topics in algebraic geometry and geometric modeling, 169–184, Contemp. Math., 334, Amer. Math. Soc., Providence, RI, 2003.

Rome: Accademia Nazionale dei Lincei (1603) in Villa Farnesina (1510). The author was invited to give a lecture here in 1978.

2004

- 2500th anniversary of the birth of **Sophocles** (c. 496 BC – c. 406 BC, aged c. 90), one of three ancient Greek tragedians (with Aeschylus (29 years older) and Euripides (11 years younger)) whose plays have survived. Quotes:

Always desire to learn something useful.
If we are to keep our democracy, there must be one commandment: "Thou shalt not ration justice."
No treaty is ever an impediment to a cheat.
There is no greater evil than anarchy.
Success is dependent on effort.
To be doing good deeds is man's most glorious task.
Who seeks shall find.
Without labor nothing prospers.
A short saying often contains much wisdom.
Fortune cannot aid those who do nothing.
One word frees us of all the weight and pain in life. That word is love.
Our happiness depends on wisdom all the way.
Silence is an ornament for women.
Time alone reveals the just man; but you might discern a bad man in a single day.
What house, bloated with luxury, ever became prosperous without a woman's excellence?
Wisdom is the supreme part of happiness.
Wisdom outweighs any wealth.
You should not consider a man's age but his acts.

- 29 April – 150th anniversary of the birth of **Jules Henri Poincaré** (29 April 1854 – 17 July 1912, aged 58.2), French mathematician, theoretical physicist, engineer, and philosopher of science. He is often described as a polymath, and in mathematics as "The Last Universalist," since he excelled in all fields of the discipline as it existed during his lifetime. One of his doctorands was Dimitrie Pompeiu (4 Oct 1873 – 8 Oct 1954, aged 81years and 4 days), renowned mathematician. Poincaré's quotes:

A small error in the former will produce an enormous error in the latter.

A very small cause, which escapes our notice, determines a considerable effect that we cannot fail to see, and then we say that the effect is due to chance.

Facts do not speak.

Ideas rose in clouds; I felt them collide until pairs interlocked, so to speak, making a stable combination.

If one looks at the different problems of the integral calculus, which arise naturally when one wishes to go deep into the different parts of physics, it is impossible not to be struck by the analogies existing.

If that enabled us to predict the succeeding situation with the same approximation, that is all we require, and we should say that the phenomenon had been predicted, that it is governed by the laws.

Invention consists in avoiding the constructing of useless contraptions, and in constructing the useful combinations, which are in infinite minority.

It is the harmony of the diverse parts, their symmetry, their happy balance; in a word it is all that introduces order, all that gives unity, that permits us to see clearly, and to comprehend at once both the ensemble and the details.

Mathematical discoveries, small or great, are never born of spontaneous generation.

Mathematicians are born, not made.

Mathematicians do not study objects, but relations between objects.

One would have to have completely forgotten the history of science, so as to not remember that the desire to know nature has had the most constant, and the happiest influence, on the development of mathematics.

Thought is only a flash between two long nights, but this flash is everything.

To doubt everything, or, to believe everything, are two equally convenient solutions; both dispense with the necessity of reflection.

- The author, 61, published his 56th to 70th reviews in the Mathematical Reviews of the American Mathematical Society, of 15 articles and books published this year, regarding algorithms for optimal multi-resolution quantization, compact roundtrip routing in directed networks, polynomials in the nation's service: using algebra to design the advanced encryption standard, on systems of linear equations with nonnegative coefficients, geometric programming duals of channel capacity and rate distortion, (the next is a book with 234 pages) Coding theory. A first course, (the next is a book with 194 pages) Multiresolution methods in scattered data modelling, number theoretical error estimates in a quantization scheme for bandlimited signals, an information-theoretic model for steganography, parametrization of approximate algebraic curves by lines, Reed-Muller expressions in the previous decade, an algorithm for parametric quadric patch construction. Geometric modelling, tensorial rational surfaces with base points via massic vectors, algebraic attacks and decomposition of Boolean functions. Chapter in Advances in cryptology—EUROCRYPT 2004, 474–491, and an elementary proof of MacWilliams-Delsarte identity.

Japan, Tokyo (1180), special ward Shinjuku, from the 45th fl., 202 m, of Tokyo Met. Gov Bg North Tower): Shinjuku Sumitomo Bldg. (210 m, 52 fl, 1974, center), Shinjuku Mitsui Building (224 m, 55 floors, 1974, right).

2005

- 2200th anniversary of the birth of **Publius Terentius Afer** (or Terence, 195 BC, Carthage (now in Tunisia) - 159 BC, Greece, aged 36), playwright of the Roman Republic

Da locum melioribus - Give way to your betters.

Amantes sunt amentes - Lovers are lunatics.

Amantium irae amoris integratio est - The anger of lovers is the renewal of love.

Quot homines tot sententiae - So many men so many questions.

Extreme law is often extreme injustice.

I am a man, and whatever concerns humanity is of interest to me.

That is true wisdom, to know how to alter one's mind when occasion demands it.

In fact nothing is said that has not been said before.

- 1950th anniversary of the birth of **Publius Cornelius Tacitus** (55 – 117, aged 62), Roman historian and senator. Quotes:

Corruptissima re publica plurimae leges - In a very corrupt state are the most laws.

A desire to resist oppression is implanted in the nature of man.

All things atrocious and shameless flock from all parts to Rome.

Prosperity is the measure or touchstone of virtue, for it is less difficult to bear misfortunes than to remain uncorrupted by pleasure.

Reason and judgment are the qualities of a leader.

Candor and generosity, unless tempered by due moderation, leads to ruin.

Custom adapts itself to expediency.

Fear is not in the habit of speaking truth; when perfect sincerity is expected, perfect freedom must be allowed; nor has anyone, who is apt to be angry when he hears the truth, any cause to wonder that he does not hear it.

Greater things are believed of those who are absent.

Love of fame is the last thing even learned men can bear to be parted from.

- The author, 62, published his 70th to 78th reviews in the Mathematical Reviews of the American Mathematical Society, of 9 articles published this year, regarding an analytic pseudo-spectral method to generate a regular 4-sided PDE surface patch, distance properties of ϵ-points on algebraic curves. Chapter in Computational methods for algebraic spline surfaces, 45–61, Springer, Berlin, 2005, Lewis Carroll's ciphers: the literary connections, optimal colored threshold visual cryptography schemes, closest points, moving surfaces, and algebraic geometry, statistical elimination of boundary artefacts in image deblurring, a nonnegatively constrained trust region algorithm for the restoration of images with an unknown blur, do all elliptic curves of the same order have the same difficulty of discrete log?, algorithm of local resolution of singularities of a space curve. Chapter in Computer algebra in scientific computing, 405–415, Lecture Notes in Comput. Sci., 3718, Springer, Berlin, 2005.

2006

- 17 January - 300th anniversary of the birth of **Benjamin Franklin** (January 17, 1706, on Milk Street in Boston, Massachusetts Bay, English America – April 17, 1790, USA, aged 84 years and 3 months), an American polymath and one of the Founding Fathers of the United States. Franklin was a leading author, printer, political theorist, politician, freemason, postmaster, scientist, inventor, humorist, civic activist, statesman, and diplomat. As a scientist he is known for his discoveries and theories regarding electricity. As an inventor, he is known for the lightning rod, bifocals, and the Franklin stove, among other inventions. He founded many civic organizations, including Philadelphia's fire department and the University of Pennsylvania. Quotes:

An investment in knowledge pays the best interest.

Remember not only to say the right thing in the right place, but, far more difficult still, to leave unsaid the wrong thing at the tempting moment.

Fatigue is the best pillow.

Be slow in choosing a friend, slower in changing.

Little strokes, fell great oaks.

- 27 January – 250th anniversary of the birth of **Wolfgang Amadeus Mozart** (27 January 1756 – 5 December 1791, aged 35.8), a prolific and very influential Austrian composer. Quotes:

My great-grandfather used to say to his wife, my great-grandmother, who in turn told her daughter, my grandmother, who repeated it to her daughter, my mother, who used to remind her daughter, my own sister, that to talk well and eloquently is a very great art, but that an equally great one is to know the right moment to stop.

When I am traveling in a carriage, or walking after a good meal, or during the night when I cannot sleep; it is on such occasions that ideas flow best and most abundantly.

I pay no attention whatever to anybody's praise or blame. I simply follow my own feelings.

Nor do I hear in my imagination the parts successively, I hear them all at once. What a delight this is! All this inventing, this producing, takes place in a pleasing, lively dream.

My subject enlarges itself, becomes methodized and define, and the whole, though it be long, stands almost complete and finished in my mind, so that I can survey it, like a fine picture or a beautiful statute, at a glance.

- 150 years ago, in 1856, the Latin adverb **sīc**, which contains a long vowel and means "so", "thus", "as such" or "in such a manner" appeared in English [*sic*], meaning "intentionally so written".

- The author, 63, published his 78th to 85th reviews in the Mathematical Reviews of the American Mathematical Society, of 8 articles and books published this year, regarding (book) A classical introduction to cryptography. Applications for communications security. Springer, New York, 2006. xviii+335 pp, acceleration schemes for computing centroidal Voronoi tessellations, a brief SNR analysis in turbo decoding and its applications, implicitization of parametric curves via Lagrange interpolation, on the use of cellular automata in symmetric cryptography, (book) Introduction to cryptography with coding theory. Second edition. Pearson Prentice Hall, Upper Saddle River, NJ, 2006. xiv+577 pp, tight bounds for unconditional authentication protocols in the manual channel and shared key models. Chapter in Advances in cryptology—CRYPTO 2006, 214–231, Lecture Notes in Comput. Sci., 4117, Springer, Berlin, 2006, and coding for the multiple-access adder channel.

Japan, Kyoto (678, it was the imperial capital of Japan for over 1,000 years): Kyoto Tower Hotel, on Shiokoji Dori, 200 m north of Kyoto Railway Station.

2007

- 20 March - 2050th anniversary of the birth of **Publius Ovidius Naso** (20 March 43 BC, Sulmo, Roman Empire (now Sulmona, Italy) – 17 AD, Tomis, Moesia, Roman Empire (now Constanța, Romania), aged circa 59), great Roman poet. Sulmo was in an Apennine valley, 120 km east of Rome, in Roman Republic (now Sulmona, in the province of L'Aquila in Abruzzo, Italy). In 8 AD, Ovidius, 50, was exiled by Augustus, 71, to Tomis, Scythia Minor, Roman Empire (now Constanța, Romania). About 9 years later he died there.

When Ovidius was born, Vergilius was 26 years 5 months and 5 days, returned to Mantova, and continued to work on the Eclogues. Horatius was 21 years, 3 months and 12 days. Ovidius' quotes:

A prince should be slow to punish, and quick to reward.

Alas! How difficult it is not to betray one's guilt by one's looks.

Bear and endure: This sorrow will one day prove to be for your good

Beauty is a fragile gift.

Blemishes are hid by night and every fault forgiven; darkness makes any woman fair.

Chance is always powerful. Let your hook always be cast; in the pool where you least expect it, there will be fish.

Courage conquers all things: it even gives strength to the body.

Enhance and intensify one's vision of that synthesis of truth and beauty which is the highest and deepest reality.

First appearance deceives many.

First thing every morning before you arise say out loud, "I believe," three times.

Fortune and love favor the brave.

Habits change into character.

Happy are those who dare courageously to defend what they love.

Happy is the man who has broken the chains which hurt the mind, and has given up worrying once and for all.

How little is the promise of the child fulfilled in the man.

If you want to be loved, be lovable.

In our leisure we reveal what kind of people we are.

Let others praise ancient times; I am glad I was born in these.

Like fragile ice anger passes away in time.

Make the workmanship surpass the materials.

Men do not value a good deed unless it brings a reward.

Minds that are ill at ease are agitated by both hope and fear.

My hopes are not always realized, but I always hope.

Neither can the wave that has passed by be recalled, nor the hour which has passed return again.

Note too that a faithful study of the liberal arts humanizes character, and permits it not to be cruel.

Nowadays nothing but money counts: a fortune brings honors, friendships; the poor man everywhere lies low.

People are slow to claim confidence in undertakings of magnitude.

Take rest; a field that has rested gives a beautiful crop.

Tears at times have the weight of speech.

The burden which is well borne becomes light.

The cause is hidden; the effect is visible to all.

The heavier crop is ever in others' fields.

Fire, though it may be quenched, will not become cool.

The man who has experienced shipwreck shudders even at a calm sea.

The sharp thorn often produces delicate roses.

The will is commendable though the ability may be wanting.

There is a god within us.

There is more refreshment and stimulation in a nap, even of the briefest, than in all the alcohol ever distilled.

There is no such thing as pure pleasure; some anxiety always goes with it.

Those things that nature denied to human sight, it revealed to the eyes of the soul.

Time is generally the best doctor.

Time is the devourer of all things.

Time, motion and wine cause sleep.

To feel our ills is one thing, but to cure them is another.
Use the occasion, for it passes swiftly.
Venus favors the bold.
What is deservedly suffered must be borne with calmness.
You will go most safely in the middle.
What is now reason was formerly impulse or instinct.
What is without periods of rest will not endure.
We have nothing that is not perishable, except what our hearts and our intellects endow us with.
You can learn from anyone, even your enemy.

- 15 April – 300th anniversary of the birth of **Leonhard Euler** (15 April 1707, Basel, Switzerland – 18 September 1783, Saint Petersburg, Russia, aged 76.4), Swiss mathematician, physicist, astronomer, logician and engineer, who made important discoveries in infinitesimal calculus and graph theory, topology and analytic number theory. He also introduced much of the modern mathematical terminology and notation, particularly for mathematical analysis, such as the notion of a mathematical function. He is also known for his work in mechanics, fluid dynamics, optics, astronomy, and music theory. Quotes
For since the fabric of the universe is most perfect and the work of a most wise Creator, nothing at all takes place in the universe in which some rule of maximum or minimum does not appear.
Mathematicians have tried in vain to this day to discover some order in the sequence of prime numbers, and we have reason to believe that it is a mystery into which the human mind will never penetrate.

- The author, 64, published his 85th to 93rd reviews in the Mathematical Reviews of the American Mathematical Society, of 9 articles and books published this year, regarding plotting missing points and branches of real parametric curves, implicitization of rational curves and polynomial surfaces, B-spline control nets for developable surfaces, an extension of Bernstein-Bézier surface over the triangular domain, inheriting thinning for skeleton-based mesh decomposition. Curve and surface design: Avignon 2006, constructions of optical orthogonal codes from finite geometry, one sketch for all: fast algorithms for compressed sensing. STOC'07—Proceedings of the 39th Annual ACM Symposium on Theory of Computing, 237–246, ACM, New York, 2007, application of non-convex BV regularization for image segmentation. Image processing based on partial differential equations, 211–228, Math. Vis., Springer, Berlin, 2007, and joint source-channel coding using real BCH codes for robust image transmission.

Japan, Osaka (645 AD, the 3rd largest city in Japan, capital of Osaka Prefecture on the main island Honshu): Toyosaki shrine (1772, with the Emperor Kotoku and others enshrined here).

Constanta, Romania, Piazza Ovidiu: Statue of Publius Ovidius Naso (20 March 43 BC, in Sulmona – 17, in Tomis, Moesia (now Constanta, Romania), aged circa 59, close to the place where Ovidius died.

2008

9 December - 400th anniversary of the birth of **John Milton** (9 Dec 1608, Bread Street, City of London, UK – 8 Nov 1674, Bunhill Row, London, UK, aged 65.9), English poet, polemicist, man of letters, and civil servant, best known for his epic poem Paradise Lost, written in blank verse. Quotes:

A good book is the precious lifeblood of a master spirit, embalmed and treasured up on purpose to a life beyond life.

Give me the liberty to know, to utter, and to argue freely according to conscience, above all liberties.

He who reigns within himself, and rules passions, desires, and fears, is more than a king.

Love-quarrels oft in pleasing concord end.

None can love freedom heartily, but good men; the rest love not freedom, but license.

The superior man acquaints himself with many sayings of antiquity and many deeds of the past, in order to strengthen his character thereby.

- The author, 65, published his 94th to 103rd reviews in the Mathematical Reviews of the American Mathematical Society, of 10 articles and books published this year, regarding coprimitive sets and inextendable codes, a general framework for surface modeling using geometric partial differential equations, nondegeneracy and weak global convergence of the Lloyd algorithm in a certain space, on the dual of a Coulter-Matthews bent function, (book) Algebraic codes on lines, planes, and curves. An engineering approach. Cambridge University Press, Cambridge, 2008. xxii+543 pp, distributed compression and multiparty squashed entanglement, doppler resilient Golay complementary waveforms, reducing lattice bases to find small-height values of univariate polynomials, a birthday paradox for Markov chains, with an optimal bound for collision in the Pollard rho algorithm for discrete logarithm. Algorithmic number theory, 402–415, Lecture Notes in Comput. Sci., 5011, Springer, Berlin, 2008, and fast solution of l1-norm minimization problems when the solution may be sparse.

London, from the Shard (2012, 309 m, observatory at 244 m), looking east to the Tower Bridge (1886-1894, combined bascule and suspension turreted bridge over River Thames (flowing from west (left) to east (right)), between London boroughs Tower Hamlets (north – left up) and Southwark (south – right), length 244 m, height 65 m, longest span 82 m, clearance 8 m (closed), 42 m (open)), City Hall (2002, height 45 m, center right round, for the Greater London Authority: Mayor of London and the London Assembly).

2009

- the 2350th anniversary of the birth of **Epicurus** (341 BC – 270 BC, aged 71), an ancient Greek philosopher who founded an influential school of philosophy, called Epicureanism. Quotes:

A free life cannot acquire many possessions, because this is not easy to do without servility to mobs or monarchs.

Do not spoil what you have by desiring what you have not; remember that what you now have was once among the things you only hoped for.

I have never wished to cater to the crowd; for what I know they do not approve, and what they approve I do not know.

If thou wilt make a man happy, add not unto his riches but take away from his desires.

It is not so much our friends' help that helps us, as the confidence of their help.

Not what we have but what we enjoy, constitutes our abundance.

Of all the things which wisdom provides to make us entirely happy, much the greatest is the possession of friendship.

Riches do not exhilarate us so much with their possession as they torment us with their loss.

The greater the difficulty, the more the glory in surmounting it.

The time when most of you should withdraw into yourself is when you are forced to be in a crowd.

- 12 February - 200th anniversary of the birth of **Abraham Lincoln** (12 Feb 1809, Hodgenville, KY, USA – 15 April 1865, Petersen House, Washington, DC, USA, aged 56.1), American statesman who served as the 16th President of the United States for 4.1 years, from 4 March 1861 (age 52) until 15 April 1865. Quotes:

All that I am, or hope to be, I owe to my angel mother.

A friend is one who has the same enemies as you have.

Always bear in mind that your own resolution to succeed is more important than any other.

America will never be destroyed from the outside. If we falter and lose our freedoms, it will be because we destroyed ourselves.

Avoid popularity if you would have peace.

Ballots are the rightful and peaceful successors to bullets.

Better to remain silent and be thought a fool than to speak out and remove all doubt.

Books serve to show a man that those original thoughts of his aren't very new at all.

You can fool all the people some of the time, and some of the people all the time, but you cannot fool all the people all the time.

You have to do your own growing, no matter how tall your grandfather was.

- 12 February - 200th anniversary of the birth of **Charles Robert Darwin**, (12 February 1809 – 19 April 1882, aged 73.2), English naturalist, geologist and biologist, best known for his contributions to the evolution theory. He had 10 children. Quotes:

It is not the strongest of the species that survive, nor the most intelligent, but the one most responsive to change.

A man who darcs to waste one hour of time has not discovered the value of life.

I have called this principle, by which each slight variation, if useful, is preserved, by the term of Natural Selection.

The highest possible stage in moral culture is when we recognize that we ought to control our thoughts.

The very essence of instinct is that it's followed independently of reason.

To kill an error is as good a service as, and sometimes even better than, the establishing of a new truth or fact.

How paramount the future is to the present when one is surrounded by children.

- The author, 66, published his 104th to 111th reviews in the Mathematical Reviews of the American Mathematical Society, of 8 articles and books published this year, regarding meshless methods for physics-based modeling and simulation of deformable models, efficient representation in spaces of plane curves, bounded variation regularization using line sections, an algorithm for finding a nearly minimal balanced set in a certain space, geometric growth and character development in large metastable networks, invariant-geometry conditions for the rational bi-quadratic Bézier surfaces, linear and nonlinear sequences and applications to stream ciphers. Recent trends in cryptography, 21–45, Contemp. Math., 477, Amer. Math. Soc., Providence, RI, 2009, and an adaptive approach for affine-invariant 2D shape description.

From the Westminster Bridge (1862) looking southwest to the Palace of Westminster (1016, 1870), Big Ben (1855, 96 m, right).

Japan, Tokyo (1180), special ward Shinjuku: Tokyo Metropolitan Government Building, 243 m, 48 floors, 1991, with two observation decks on floor 45, at 202 m.

Chapter 6. 2010 - 2019

2010

- 200 years ago, in 1810, Antonio Canova (1757 – 1822, aged 65, sculptor from Venezia) finished Venere (Venus) Italica, a carved Carrara marble sculpture, 1.75 m, commissioned by Napoleon Bonaparte (1769 – 1821, aged 52).

- 200th anniversary of the birth of Frédéric Chopin (1810-1849, aged 39).

- The author, 67, published his 112th to 123rd reviews in the Mathematical Reviews of the American Mathematical Society, of 12 articles and books published this year, regarding approximate parametrization of plane algebraic curves by linear systems of curves, classification of convolutional codes, spatio-temporal speckle reduction in ultrasound sequences, linear precision for parametric patches, on rational Minkowski Pythagorean hodograph curves, a new hybrid descent method with application to the optimal design of finite precision FIR filters, improving the high order nonlinearity lower bound for Boolean functions with given algebraic immunity, scroll codes over curves of higher genus, constructing implicit curves based on guidance vectors, a novel curvature estimator for digital curves and images. Pattern recognition, 442–451, Lecture Notes in Comput. Sci., 6376, Springer, Berlin, 2010, symmetries and groups in signal processing, and (book) An introduction. Signals and Communication Technology. Springer, Dordrecht, 2010. xii+160 pp.

Venere (Venus) Italica, 1810, by Antonio Canova (1757 – 1822, aged 65, sculptor from Venezia), a carved Carrara marble sculpture, 1.75 m, commissioned by Napoleon Bonaparte (1769 – 1821, aged 52).

2011

– 1800th anniversary of the birth of **Diophantus of Alexandria** (211 – 295, aged 84), mathematician, who was the author of a series of books called Arithmetica, many of which are now lost. He is called "the father of algebra".

- 500 years ago, in 1511, Michelangelo, 36, completed The Creation of Man (1510-1511), a fresco on the vault of the Sistine Chapel.

25 October – 200th anniversary of the birth of **Évariste Galois** (25 October 1811 – 31 May 1832, aged 20.6), great French mathematician. While still in his teens, he was able to determine a necessary and sufficient condition for a polynomial to be solvable by radicals, thereby solving a problem standing for 350 years. His work laid the foundations for Galois theory and group theory, two major branches of abstract algebra, and the subfield of Galois connections.

- The author, 68, published his 124th to 138th reviews in the Mathematical Reviews of the American Mathematical Society, of 15 articles and books published this year, regarding an entropy based theory of the grain boundary character distribution, adaptive skin meshes coarsening for biomolecular simulation, composite cyclotomic Fourier transforms with reduced complexities, a discrete optimization method based on a parameterization of a Grassmannian in multidimensional dichotomous data structuring, a new watermarking algorithm based on entropy concept, the Burbea-Rao and Bhattacharyya centroids, image inpainting based on coherence transport with adapted distance functions, some new constructions of authentication codes with arbitration and multi-receiver from singular symplectic geometry, structured compressed sensing: from theory to applications, jointly optimal source power control and relay matrix design in multipoint-to-multipoint cooperative communication networks, the elastic ratio: introducing curvature into ratio-based image segmentation, image magnification using interval information, hybrid wavelet denoising procedure of discontinuous surfaces, on the differential security of multivariate public key cryptosystems. Post-quantum cryptography, 130–142, Lecture Notes in Comput. Sci., 7071, Springer, Heidelberg, 2011, and When the sky falls on your head. (Italian) Mathematics and culture 2011 (Italian), 97–109, Springer Italia, Milan, 2011.

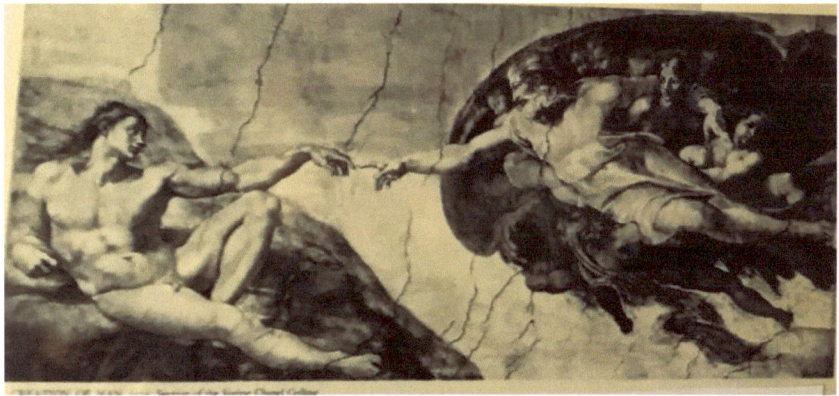

Michelangelo, 36, completed The Creation of Man (1510-1511), a fresco on the vault of the Sistine Chapel. The Lord's gesture is superb, as His mighty arm becomes the channel for the life force. Adam's arm resting passively on his knee. These two figures are the best known of all Sistine paintings.

2012

- 28 June - 300th anniversary of the birth of **Jean-Jacques Rousseau** (28 June 1712 – 2 July 1778, aged 66 years and 4 days, Genevan philosopher, writer and composer). Quotes:

A feeble body weakens the mind.

All of my misfortunes come from having thought too well of my fellows.

Falsehood has an infinity of combinations, but truth has only one mode of being.

Force does not constitute right... obedience is due only to legitimate powers.

God made me and broke the mold.

Happiness: a good bank account, a good cook, and a good digestion.

However great a man's natural talent may be, the act of writing cannot be learned all at once.

I have always said and felt that true enjoyment cannot be described.

I long remained a child, and I am still one in many respects.

I undertake the same project as Montaigne, but with an aim contrary to his own: for he wrote his Essays only for others, and I write my reveries only for myself.

Insults are the arguments employed by those who are in the wrong.

It is too difficult to think nobly, when one thinks only of earning a living.

Man was born free, and he is everywhere in chains.

Most nations, as well as people, are impossible only in their youth; they become incorrigible as they grow older.

Nature never deceives us; it is we who deceive ourselves.

No man has any natural authority over his fellow men.

- The author, 69, published his 139th to 148th reviews in the Mathematical Reviews of the American Mathematical Society, of 10 articles and books published this year, regarding an effective classification framework for brain-computer interfacing based on a combinatoric setting, THz-TDS signal analysis and substance identification via the conformal split, wavelet-based de-noising of positron emission tomography scans, an algebraic approach to reverse engineering finite dynamical systems arising from biology, Riemannian optimization on tensor products of Grassmann manifolds: applications to generalized Rayleigh-quotients, a new approach for data transmission system on topological surfaces, topological localization via signals of opportunity, reducing factorization of a semiprime number to the integration of highly oscillatory functions, magnification of label maps with a topology-preserving level-set method, and (book) Classical and quantum information. Elsevier/Academic Press, Amsterdam, 2012. xviii+725 pp.

London: from the west end of Westminster Bridge (1862) looking northwest to a horse bronze statue (1883, erected 1902) with Boadicea (circa 10 – 61) on a Roman chariot, by Thomas Thornycroff (1815-1885).

2013

- 2300th anniversary of the birth of **Archimedes** (287 BC – 212 BC, aged 75), important Greek mathematician. At 17, in 270 BC, Archimedes, after discovering the water buoyancy theories, said:

Eureka! (I have found it!)

In 269 BC, Archimedes, 18, traveled to Alexandria to study – in the same year he invented π. After 6 years, in 263 BC, Archimedes, 24, returned to Syracuse. His inventions Archimedes Claw (213 BC), screw (265 BC), and water buoyancy theories, are developed between 270 BC and 213 BC, when he was 17 to 74. 137 years after the death of Archimedes, in 75 BC, Marcus Tullius Cicero (3 Jan 106 BC – 7 Dec 43 BC, aged 63.9, Roman statesman, orator, and philosopher, who served as consul in the year 63 BC) discovered and restored Archimedes' tomb. Archimedes' quote:

Give me a lever long enough, and a fulcrum on which to place it, and I shall move the world.

Don't disturb my circles.

There are things which seem incredible to most men who have not studied Mathematics.

- The author, 70, published his 149th to 161st reviews in the Mathematical Reviews of the American Mathematical Society, of 13 articles and books published this year, regarding biarcs and bilens, unscented Kalman filtering on Riemannian manifolds, floating tangents for approximating spatial curves with G1 piecewise helices, parameterizing rational offset canal surfaces via rational contour curves, (book) Studying stellar rotation and convection. Theoretical background and seismic diagnostics. Edited by Mariejo Goupil, Kévin Belkacem, Coralie Neiner, Francois Lignières and John J. Green. Lecture Notes in Physics, 865. Springer, Heidelberg, 2013. xii+261 pp, an algorithm to parametrize approximately space curves, cooperative cognitive networks: optimal, distributed and low-complexity algorithms, the computation of previously inaccessible digits of $π^2$ and Catalan's constant, theoretic bounds to information transmission through electrical circuits, analysis of the Schrödinger operator in the context of graph characterization, encoding binary neural codes in networks of threshold-linear neurons, hybrid regularization for MRI reconstruction with static field inhomogeneity correction, and transcriptional oscillators.

London: from the Abingdon St., looking southeast to the west façade of the House of Lords of the Palace of Westminster, with the Old Palace Yard, and the equestrian statue of the King Richard I of England (Coeur de Lion or the Lionheart (1157-1199, King 1189-1199, left)).

2014

- 400 years ago, in 1614, John Napier, 64, (1550 – 4 April 1617, aged 67; Scottish mathematician, physicist, and astronomer. His Latinized name was Ioannes Neper) published Mirifici Logarithmorum Canonis Descriptio, the first table of logarithms.

- The author, 71, published his 162nd to 188st reviews in the Mathematical Reviews of the American Mathematical Society, of 27 articles and books published this year, regarding approximating Cornu spirals by arc splines, multiscale geometric modeling of macromolecules I: Cartesian representation, multiple synchronization transitions in scale-free neuronal networks with electrical and chemical hybrid synapses, on the dispersions of three network information theory problems, an octahedral equal area partition of the sphere and near optimal configurations of points, optimal chaotic desynchronization for neural populations, computation with no memory, and rearrangeable multicast networks, collaborative 20 questions for target localization, sub-Nyquist radar via Doppler focusing, an improved sub-packetization bound for minimum storage regenerating codes, stable restoration and separation of approximately sparse signals, robust dequantized compressive sensing, a theory of network equivalence—Part II: Multiterminal channels, stable length estimates of tube-like shapes, a new tangentially stabilized 3D curve evolution algorithm and its application in virtual colonoscopy, generic models in ensemble of scalar field cosmology—toward selection of a form of potential of scalar field, hidden cliques and the certification of the restricted isometry property, on network functional compression, Big Bang, blowup, and modular curves: algebraic geometry in cosmology, cognitive Wyner networks with clustered decoding, thermodynamic semirings, gravity effects of polyhedral bodies with linearly varying density, spiral galaxy lensing: a model with twist, a cell population model structured by cell age incorporating cell-cell adhesion. Mathematical oncology 2013, 109–149, successive cancellation decoding of Reed-Solomon codes, minimum number of edges in a hypergraph guaranteeing a perfect fractional matching and the MMS conjecture, and properties of subentropy.

At the Royal Observatory Greenwich (1676), the official Greenwich Mean Time (GMT was replaced by Coordinated Universal Time (UTC) in 1960) on the Shepherd 24-hour gate galvano-magnetic clock (10:21:42), public standards of length for British yard (0.9144 m), two feet (0.6096 m), one foot (0.3048 m), six inches (0.1524 m), three inches (0.0762 m, down), height above mean sea level 154.7 feet (47.15 m, on the plaque in the center up).

2015

- 2500th anniversary of the birth of **Euripides** (c. 485 BC, Salamis Island, Greece – 406 BC, Macedonia, aged 79), tragedian of classical Athens. Along with Aeschylus (40 years older) and Sophocles (11 years older, but they died in the same year), he is one of the three ancient Greek tragedians for whom a significant number of plays have survived (over 90). Quotes:
 Friends show their love in times of trouble, not in happiness.
 One loyal friend is worth ten thousand relatives.
 Talk sense to a fool and he calls you foolish.
 When a good man is hurt, all who would be called good must suffer with him.
 To a father growing old nothing is dearer than a daughter.
 Experience, travel — these are an education in themselves.
 Love makes the time pass. Time makes love pass.

- 1 April - 200th anniversary of the birth of Otto Eduard Leopold, Prince of Bismarck, Duke of Lauenburg, known as **Otto von Bismarck** (1 April 1815, Schönhausen, Germany – 30 July 1898, Friedrichsruh, Aumühle, Germany, aged 83.3), Prussian statesman who dominated German and European affairs from the 1860s until 1890, and was the first Chancellor of the German Empire for 19 years, between 1871 and 1890. Quotes:
 All treaties between great states cease to be binding when they come in conflict with the struggle for existence.
 The secret of politics? Make a good treaty with Russia.
 People never lie so much as before an election, during a war, or after a hunt.
 Politics is the art of the possible.
 The main thing is to make history, not to write it.
 Politics ruins the character.
 When you want to fool the world, tell the truth.
 Never believe anything in politics until it has been officially denied.

- The author, 72, published his 189th to 222nd reviews in the Mathematical Reviews of the American Mathematical Society, of 34 articles and books published this year, regarding block coherence of frames, (book) Neurons—a mathematical ignition. Series on Number Theory and its Applications, 9. World Scientific Publishing Co. Pte. Ltd., Hackensack, NJ, 2015. xiv+216 pp, Pareto-depth for multiple-query image retrieval, three derivative-free projection methods for nonlinear equations with convex constraints, sampling, metric entropy, and dimensionality reduction, robust multiple signal classification via probability measure transformation, numerical analysis of a hyperbolic hemivariational inequality arising in dynamic contact, non-local Retinex—a unifying framework and beyond, adaptive search and tracking of sparse dynamic targets under resource constraints, regularized solution of LCP problems with application to rigid body dynamics, Abelian group codes for channel coding and source coding, tractable diffusion and coalescent processes for weakly correlated loci, manifold learning for latent variable inference in dynamical systems, (book) Sparse approximation with bases. Edited by Sergey Tikhonov. Advanced Courses in Mathematics. CRM Barcelona. Birkhäuser/Springer, Basel, 2015. xii+261 pp, primal-dual active set methods for large-scale optimization, symmetric polynomials in information theory: entropy and subentropy, a posteriori error identities for nonlinear variational problems, bent vectorial functions and linear codes from o-polynomials, a weighted difference of anisotropic and isotropic total variation model for image processing, convergence rate analysis of primal-dual splitting schemes, deep community detection, robust linear spectral unmixing using anomaly detection, on convex finite-dimensional variational methods in imaging sciences and Hamilton-Jacobi equations, a measure of dependence for cryptographic primitives relative to ideal functions, importance-weighted adaptive search for multi-class targets, convergence rate of some hybrid multigrid methods for variational inequalities, real-time adaptive video compression, spectral correlation hub screening of multivariate time series, a spectral analysis approach for experimental designs, a predictor-corrector algorithm for monotone linear complementarity problems in a wide neighborhood, noise-shaping quantization methods for frame-based and compressive sampling systems, a sheaf-theoretic perspective on sampling, (book) Machine learning for audio, image and video analysis. Theory and applications. Second edition. Advanced Information and Knowledge Processing. Springer, London, 2015. xvi+561 pp, and (book in 3 volumes) Photons in Fock space and beyond. Vol. I. From classical to quantized radiation systems. Vol. II. Quantized mesoscopic radiation models. Vol. III. Mathematics for photon fields. World Scientific Publishing Co. Pte. Ltd., Hackensack, NJ, 2015. xxxvii+2084+L pp.

The north side of the Royal Observatory (1676), and the 38-inch (965.2 mm) Telescope Dome (left up), and meridian 0 to the right.

2016

2500th anniversary of the birth of **Herodotus** (c. 484 BC, Halicarnassus, Persian Empire – 425 BC, Thurii, Greece (now Italy), aged 59), ancient Greek historian who wrote the book The Histories, a detailed record of his study on the origins of the Greco-Persian Wars. Quotes:

Force has no place where there is need of skill.

If a man insisted always on being serious, and never allowed himself a bit of fun and relaxation, he would go mad or become unstable without knowing it.

Illness strikes men when they are exposed to change.

The only good is knowledge, and the only evil is ignorance.

To think well, and to consent to obey someone giving good advice, are the same thing.

Circumstances rule men; men do not rule circumstances.

I am bound to tell what I am told, but not in every case to believe it.

It is clear that not in one thing alone, but in many ways equality and freedom of speech are a good thing.

It's impossible for someone who is human to have all good things together, just as there is no single country able to provide all good things for itself.

The most hateful human misfortune is for a wise man to have no influence.

Great deeds are usually wrought at great risks.

Great things are won by great dangers.

He is the best man who, when making his plans, fears and reflects on everything that can happen to him, but in the moment of action is bold.

Knowledge may give weight, but accomplishments give luster, and many more people see than weigh.

Some men give up their designs when they have almost reached the goal; while others, on the contrary, obtain a victory by exerting, at the last moment, more vigorous efforts than ever before.

The man who has planned badly, if fortune is on his side, may have had a stroke of luck; but his plan was a bad one nonetheless.

Men trust their ears less than their eyes.

Of all men's miseries the bitterest is this: to know so much and to have control over nothing.

Of all possessions, a friend is the most precious.

2400th anniversary of the birth of **Aristotle** (384 BC – 2 Oct 322 BC, aged 62), great Greek philosopher and scientist, student of Plato (43 years older than Aristotle), teacher of Alexander the Great (20 July 356 BC – 10 June 323 BC, aged 32 years 10 months and 21 days, 28 years younger than Aristotle; Alexander's empire was the largest state of its time, covering approximately 5.2 millions of km^2 (Greece, Turkey, Iraq, Iran, Afghanistan, Pakistan and half of Egypt (which, in total, is more than half of the U.S.))). Quotes:

It is the mark of an educated mind to be able to entertain a thought without accepting it.

The roots of education are bitter, but the fruit is sweet.

It is the mark of an educated mind to rest satisfied with the degree of precision, which the nature of the subject admits, and not to seek exactness, where only an approximation is possible.

Nature does nothing uselessly.

Teaching is the highest form of understanding.

The secret to humor is surprise.

- The author, 73, published his 223rd to 238th reviews in the Mathematical Reviews of the American Mathematical Society, of 16 articles and books published this year, regarding secondary Laplace operator and generalized Giaquinta-Hildebrandt operator with applications on surface segmentation and smoothing, numerical methods for genetic regulatory network identification based on a variational approach, biochemical reaction networks: an invitation for algebraic geometers. Chapter in Mathematical Congress of the Americas, 65–83, Contemp. Math., 656, Amer. Math. Soc., Providence, RI, 2016, (book) Hiding data—selected topics. Rudolf Ahlswede's lectures on information theory. 3. Foundations in Signal Processing, Communications and

Networking, 12. Springer, [Cham], 2016. xiv+356 pp, on a mathematical theory of coded exposure, numerical methods for the Stokes and Navier-Stokes equations driven by threshold slip boundary conditions, (book) Calculating the cosmos. How mathematics unveils the universe. Basic Books, New York, 2016. 320 pp, one-bit compressed sensing by greedy algorithms, compressed sensing recovery via nonconvex shrinkage penalties, distributed noise-shaping quantization: I. Beta duals of finite frames and near-optimal quantization of random measurements, weighted Lupaş q-Bézier curves, off-the-grid recovery of piecewise constant images from few Fourier samples, exploring structured sparsity by a reweighted Laplace prior for hyperspectral compressive sensing, (book) Abstract methods in information theory. Second edition. Series on Multivariate Analysis, 10. World Scientific Publishing Co. Pte. Ltd., Hackensack, NJ, 2016. xiv+398 pp, two extensions of the Dai-Liao method with sufficient descent property based on a penalization scheme, and weakly chained diagonally dominant B-matrices and error bounds for linear complementarity problems.

Japan, Kyoto (678, it was the imperial capital of Japan for over 1,000 years): Kyoto Central Post Office, north-west of Kyoto Railway Station.

2017

15 November - at a Christie's auction in New York, Leonardo da Vinci's painting Salvator Mundi (finished by him in 1500, when he was 48) was sold, after 517 years, for a world record of $450.3 M, the highest price ever paid for a work of art.

- 14 December – After 2009 years, Rome city council overturned banishment of 'one of the greatest poets', after Augustus forced him to leave on the year 8 AD. Therefore, 2009 years after Augustus banished him to Tomis, on the Black Sea (now Constanța, Romania), the poet Ovidius has been rehabilitated.
Rome city council on Thursday, 14 Dec 2017, unanimously approved a motion tabled by the M5S party to "repair the serious wrong" suffered by Ovidius, thought of as one of the three canonical poets of Latin literature, along with Vergilius and Horatius.
Best known for his 15-book epic narrative poem Metamorphoses, and the elegy Ars Amatoria, or the Art of Love, Publius Ovidius Naso was exiled in 8 AD to Tomis, the ancient Black Sea settlement now known as the Romanian port city of Constanța.
He remained there until his death, about 9 years later. Although ordered directly by the emperor, scholars have long speculated over the motive for Ovidius' exile; the poet himself attributed it to "carmen et error", a poem and a mistake.
Experts believe the cause was probably a combination of three factors: that Ovidius' erotic poetry was considered offensive, his attitude to Augustus was too disrespectful, and that he may have been involved in an unspecified plot or scandal. In my view, the reason is that Ovidius was close to Augustus's family, especially to grandson Agrippa Postumus, now 20 and exiled for antisocial behavior, to granddaughter Julia the Younger, 27, also banished (for having an affair with a senator), and to her husband Lucius Aemilius Paullus (37 BC – 8, aged 45), who was executed as a conspirator in a plot against Augustus – it seems that Ovidius new about this plot, but did not inform Augustus.
Sulmona, the Abruzzo town where the poet was born (then Sulmo), formally acquitted him of any wrongdoing. Dante Alighieri (30 May 1265, Firenze, Italy – 14 Sep 1321, Ravenna, Italy, aged 56.3), the

great Renaissance poet, was similarly pardoned, after 706 years, in 2008 by Firenze (Florence) – from where he was exiled on pain of death in 1302 (he was 37).

- The author, 74, published his 239th to 252nd reviews in the Mathematical Reviews of the American Mathematical Society, of 14 articles and books published this year, regarding learning to classify with possible sensor failures, a relaxation modulus-based matrix splitting iteration method for solving linear complementarity problems, nonlinearly preconditioned semismooth Newton methods for variational inequality solution of two-phase flow in porous media, sparsity-inducing variational shape partitioning, (book) Foundations of quantum theory. From classical concepts to operator algebras. Fundamental Theories of Physics, 188. Springer, Cham, 2017. xv+881 pp, Polyhedral Omega: a new algorithm for solving linear Diophantine systems, mathematical modeling of equatorial atmospheric waves similar to those travelling along a hexagon-shaped path at the north pole of Saturn, (book) Rigorous time slicing approach to Feynman path integrals. Mathematical Physics Studies. Springer, Tokyo, 2017. ix+333 pp, parallel and cyclic hybrid subgradient extragradient methods for variational inequalities, overview of shelling for 2-manifold surface reconstruction based on 3D Delaunay triangulation, (book) Quantum continuous variables. A primer of theoretical methods. CRC Press, Boca Raton, FL, 2017. xviii+349 pp, quadratic convergence of monotone iterates for semilinear elliptic obstacle problems, (book) Quantum theory, groups and representations. An introduction. Springer, Cham, 2017. xxii+668 pp, and (book) Non-relativistic quantum mechanics. Cambridge University Press, Cambridge, 2017. xvii+438 pp.

On Gagarin (First Man in Space) Terrace, on the southwest part of the South Building (1899) of the Royal Observatory Greenwich (1676), looking northeast to the south part of the west side (right), the west part of the south side (left), and to the statue of Yuri Gagarin (1934-1968, Russian cosmonaut, the first man to journey into space, with Vostok spacecraft, which completed an orbit (1h 48') of the Earth on 12 April 1961. Resting place: Kremlin Wall Necropolis).

2018

- 23 September – 500 years ago, in 1518, College of Physicians was founded in London.

- 500 years ago, in 1518, Henricus Grammateus publishes "Ayn neu Kunstlich Buech" in Vienna, containing the earliest printed use of plus and minus signs for arithmetic.

- 6 November – the author is 75. Dediu's quote:
In order to gain wisdom, and therefore to be closer to happiness, vitam mutaveris saepe in meliores actus (change your life often for the better).

- The author, 75, published his 253rd to 265th reviews in the Mathematical Reviews of the American Mathematical Society, of 13 articles and books published this year, regarding (book) Combinatorial methods and models. Rudolf Ahlswede's lectures on information theory. 4. Foundations in Signal Processing, Communications and Networking, 13. Springer, Cham, 2018. xviii+385 pp., convex optimization approach to signals with fast varying instantaneous frequency, curve and surface fitting models based on the diagonalizable differential systems, strong convergence results for variational inequalities and fixed point problems using modified viscosity implicit rules, a mathematical theory of deep convolutional neural networks for feature extraction, learning the geometry of common latent variables using alternating-diffusion, provable approximation properties for deep neural networks, a unified framework for harmonic analysis of functions on directed graphs and changing data, image extrapolation for the time discrete metamorphosis model: existence and applications, deep convolutional framelets: a general deep learning framework for inverse problems, a Levenberg-Marquardt method for nonlinear complementarity problems based on nonmonotone trust region and line search techniques, compression algorithm for implicit 3D B-spline solids, and energy propagation in deep convolutional neural networks.

Chicago (1833): Elysées Condominiums (left, 1972, 56 floors, 161 m), Old Water Tower (left down, 1869, 47 m), 900 North Michigan (center right, 1989, 66 fl, 265 m), One Magnificent Mile (right, 1983, 57 fl, 205 m).

2019

- about 400 years ago, in France a new expression appears:
À bon entendeur, salut! (To a good listener, hello!)
The significance of this expression is: who is interested, hear or listen up. Purposely, the expression is used in original, to attract the audience's attention, with the understanding that there is much more to the matter, which cannot be said completely. Example: Now, I want to briefly say something important! À bon entendeur, salut!

Some of author's quotes:
Ad praesens amet qui nunquam amavit; quique amavit, ad praesens amet - May he love today who has never loved before; and may he who has loved, love today as well.

Few people know,
How much you have to know,
To know,
How little you know.

The most important thing on Earth is The Sun.
How many years are in your life matters, but how much life is in your years really makes your mark.
Loving is the highest form of living.
There is imperfection in everything, the question is how much.
When there is progress in some areas, the people must work very hard not to have regress in some other areas.
The Sun is much more vital than we think, and it has many more millions of surprises.
The Sun is a necessary condition for life on Earth, but not sufficient.
For good health: buy healthy foods, cook them properly, and eat them abstemiously.
The roots of many diseases essentially are in the genes.
Negative thinking is permanent; positive thinking is a rara avis (rare bird), and is very healthy.

Solutions for many problems can be found with mathematical analysis and medical help.

All the bad things done by people have a medical explanation.

The bad people need medical help, not prison. From prisons they usually come out worse. From specialized hospitals, there is a chance to cure them, and then they will pay the bill for treatment.

Your age is important, but more important is your life expectancy.

Achievement is not permanent success, but how fast you recover from a fiasco.

Much can be learned from accomplishments, but even more from fiascos.

Good achievers know to divide difficult projects in manageable small tasks.

Always the mediocrities, and their banalities, dominate. Always!

If you notice that you go in a wrong direction, the sooner you turn back, the better.

If you work hard, in a good direction, with a clear and useful objective, the success will suddenly find you.

If you categorically want to do a good task, that's passion, not work.

The more passion you have, the greater achiever you'll be.

Logic and imagination go hand in hand for great achievers.

Those who want to have great achievements don't schedule meetings, they work.

To be creative, do not follow others on their paths; create instead your own path.

For achievement one needs a good direction, hard work, persistence, tenacity, and the will to never give up.

When you have many tasks in front of you, start with the hardest one, the others will smoothly follow.

Some failures and errors are inevitable; use them to learn and improve.

Good achievers need reliable feedback from their teams; for this they cultivate an atmosphere of trust and collaboration.

It is good to offer the people what they want, but it is much better to offer them something better.

The loudness and aggressiveness are invers proportional to the intelligence and reason.

Your contacts and friends describe you.

Arrogance and self-importance are everywhere, modesty is a rara avis (rare bird).

In life try to help yourself, your family, your friends and others. When you cannot help much, just do not create problems.

It is very easy to be pessimist; choose the difficult one, and be optimist.

Loyalty comes from intense liking and appreciation.

Money is a part of happiness, but not the most important.

Common sense is essential for success, and education helps.

A strong family, with father, mother and their children, is the foundation of any good country. Without this foundation, any country will disappear.

One way to achieve success is to do what you like, you know well and it is useful for many people.

Dediu - Triumph causes self-righteousness.

Self-righteousness causes laziness.

Laziness causes fiasco.

Time is so precious and so little; you never know when it's gone.

Be hungrier for knowledge than for food.

Even a drop of education can change the color of an ocean of ignorance.

Computers are tools for education, not substitutes of it.

If we are over 30, we should ask not what our parents can do for us, but what we can do for our parents.

Happiness comes when you do good things for you, your family, your friends and many others.

Creativity comes from observation, knowledge and thinking at square.

Innovation is applied creativity.
Science and technology are the engines of progress.
The Internet is like a huge library – keep it clean and unpolluted.
The space and time are infinite.

London's only planetarium bronze cone (the largest in the world, 250 welded plates). The cone is sliced at angle parallel to celestial equator, the line on the slice is north (left, perpendicular) south (up) is parallel to 0 meridian, angle of the southern side (right) is equal to the latitude of Royal Observatory Greenwich 51° 22' 44" N.

Bibliography

"The Histories" by Polybius
"Discours de la Méthode" by René Descartes
"Meditationes de prima philosophia" by René Descartes
"Philosophiae Naturalis Principia Mathematica" by Isaac Newton
Chinese encyclopedia Gujin Tushu Jicheng (Imperial Enciclopaedia)
"Encyclopédie" by Jean-Baptiste le Rond d'Alembert and Denis Diderot
"Encyclopaedia Britannica" by over 4,400 contributors
"Unpublished Scientific Papers of Isaac Newton", the University Library, Cambridge, UK
"Encyclopedia Americana" by Francis Lieber
"Grand Larousse encyclopédique en 24 volumes" by Albert Ducrocq
"Great Russian Encyclopedia" by Yury Osipov
"Encyclopedia of China"
"Enciclopedia Italiana di Scienze, Lettere ed Arti" (35 volume), by Giovanni Treccani
"Allgemeine Encyclopädie der Wissenschaften und Künste" by Johann Samuel Ersch und Johann Gottfried Gruber
"Gran Enciclopedia de España"

Michael M. Dediu is also the author of these books (which can be found on Amazon.com):

1. Aphorisms and quotations – with examples and explanations
2. Axioms, aphorisms and quotations – with examples and explanations
3. 100 Great Personalities and their Quotations
4. Professor Petre P. Teodorescu – A Great Mathematician and Engineer
5. Professor Ioan Goia – A Dedicated Engineering Professor

6. Venice (Venezia) – a new perspective. A short presentation with photographs
7. La Serenissima (Venice) - a new photographic perspective. A short presentation with many photos
8. Grand Canal – Venice. A new photographic viewpoint. A short presentation with many photos
9. Piazza San Marco – Venice. A different photographic view. A short presentation with many photos
10. Roma (Rome) - La Città Eterna. A new photographic view. A short presentation with many photos
11. Why is Rome so Fascinating? A short presentation with many photos
12. Rome, Boston and Helsinki. A short photographic presentation
13. Rome and Tokyo – two captivating cities. A short photographic presentation
14. Beautiful Places on Earth – A new photographic presentation
15. From Niagara Falls to Mount Fuji via Rome - A novel photographic presentation
16. From the USA and Canada to Italy and Japan - A fresh photographic presentation
17. Paris – Why So Many Call This City Mon Amour - A lovely photographic presentation
18. The City of Light – Paris (La Ville-Lumière) - A kaleidoscopic photographic presentation
19. Paris (Lutetia Parisiorum) – the romance capital of the world - A kaleidoscopic photographic view
20. Paris and Tokyo – a joyful photographic presentation. With a preamble about the Universe
21. From USA to Japan via Canada – A cheerful photographic documentary
22. 200 Wonderful Places, In The Last 50 Years – A personal photographic documentary
23. Must see places in USA and Japan - A kaleidoscopic photographic documentary
24. Grandeurs of the World - A kaleidoscopic photographic documentary
25. Corneliu Leu – writer on the same wavelength as Mark Twain. An American viewpoint

26. From Berkeley to Pompeii via Rome – A kaleidoscopic photographic documentary
27. From America to Europe via Japan - A kaleidoscopic photographic documentary
28. Discover America and Japan - A photographic documentary
29. J. R. Lucas – philosopher on a creative parallel with Plato, An American viewpoint
30. From America to Switzerland via France - A photographic documentary
31. From Bretton Woods to New York via Cape Cod - A photographic documentary
32. Splendid Places on the Atlantic Coast of the U. S. A. - A photographic documentary
33. Fourteen nice Cities on three Continents - A photographic documentary
34. 17 Picturesque Cities on the World Map - A photographic documentary
35. Unforgettable Places from Four Continents including Trump buildings - A photographic documentary
36. Dediu Newsletter, Volume 1, Number 1, 6 December 2016 – Monthly news, review, comments and suggestions for a better and wiser world
37. Dediu Newsletter, Volume 1, Number 2, 6 January 2017 (available at www.derc.com).
38. Dediu Newsletter, Volume 1, Number 3, 6 February 2017 (available at www.derc.com).
39. London and Greenwich, A photographic documentary
40. Dediu Newsletter, Volume 1, Number 4, 6 March 2017 (available also at www.derc.com).
41. Dediu Newsletter, Volume 1, Number 5, 6 April 2017 (available also at www.derc.com).
42. Dediu Newsletter, Volume 1, Number 6, 6 May 2017 (available also at www.derc.com).
43. Dediu Newsletter, Volume 1, Number 7, 6 June 2017 (available also at www.derc.com).
44. London, Oxford and Cambridge, A photographic documentary
45. Dediu Newsletter, Volume 1, Number 8, 6 July 2017 (available also at www.derc.com).

46. Dediu Newsletter, Volume 1, Number 9, 6 August 2017 (available also at www.derc.com).
47. Dediu Newsletter, Volume 1, Number 10, 6 September 2017 (available also at www.derc.com).
48. Three Great Professors: President Woodrow Wilson, Historian Germán Arciniegas, Mathematician Gheorghe Vrănceanu, A chronological and photographic documentary
49. Dediu Newsletter, Volume 1, Number 11, 6 October 2017 (available also at www.derc.com).
50 Dediu Newsletter, Volume 1, Number 12, 6 November 2017 (available also at www.derc.com).
51 Dediu Newsletter, Volume 2, Number 1 (13), 6 December 2017 (available also at www.derc.com).
52 Two Great Leaders: Augustus and George Washington, A chronological and photographic documentary
53. Dediu Newsletter, Volume 2, Number 2 (14), 6 January 2018 (available also at www.derc.com).
54. Newton, Benjamin Franklin, and Gauss, A chronological and photographic documentary
55. Dediu Newsletter, Volume 2, Number 3 (15), 6 February 2018 (available also at www.derc.com).
56. 2017: World Top Events, But Many Little Known, A chronological and photographic documentary
57. Dediu Newsletter, Volume 2, Number 4 (16), 6 March 2018 (available also at www.derc.com).
58. Vergilius, Horatius, Ovidius, and Shakespeare, A chronological and photographic documentary.
59. Dediu Newsletter, Volume 2, Number 5 (17), 6 April 2018 (available also at www.derc.com).
60. Dediu Newsletter, Volume 2, Number 6 (18), 6 May 2018 (available also at www.derc.com).
61. Vivaldi, Bach, Mozart, and Verdi, A chronological and photographic documentary
62. Dediu Newsletter, Volume 2, Number 7 (19), 6 June 2018 (available also at www.derc.com).
63. Dediu Newsletter, Volume 2, Number 8 (20), 6 July 2018 (available also at www.derc.com).
64. Dediu Newsletter, Volume 2, Number 9 (21), 6 August 2018 (available also at www.derc.com).

65. World History, a new perspective - A chronological and photographic documentary.
66. World Humor History with over 100 Jokes, a new perspective - A chronological and photographic documentary
67. Dediu Newsletter, Vol 2, N 10 (22), 6 September 2018
68. Dediu Newsletter, Vol 2, N 11 (23), 6 October 2018
69. Dediu Newsletter, Vol 2, N 12 (24), 6 November 2018
70. Da Vinci, Michelangelo, Rembrandt, Rodin - A chronological and photographic documentary
71. Dediu Newsletter, Vol 3, N 1 (25), 6 December 2018
72. Dediu Newsletter, Vol 3, N 2 (26), 6 January 2019

Rome (753 BC), the goddess Diana (1590, the symbol of Chastity, by Domenico Fontana) is one (in the north) of the Quatro Fontane (the four Fountains: River Tiber, River Arno, goddess Juno) at the intersection of Via del Quirinale and Via delle Quatro Fontane

Michael M. Dediu is the editor of these books (also on Amazon.com):

1. Sophia Dediu: The life and its torrents – Ana. In Europe around 1920
2. Proceedings of the 4th International Conference "Advanced Composite Materials Engineering" COMAT 2012
3. Adolf Shvedchikov: I am an eternal child of spring – poems in English, Italian, French, German, Spanish and Russian
4. Adolf Shvedchikov: Life's Enigma – poems in English, Italian and Russian
5. Adolf Shvedchikov: Everyone wants to be HAPPY – poems in English, Spanish and Russian
6. Adolf Shvedchikov: My Life, My Love – poems in English, Italian and Russian
7. Adolf Shvedchikov: I am the gardener of love – poems in English and Russian
8. Adolf Shvedchikov: Amaretta di Saronno – poems in English and Russian
9. Adolf Shvedchikov: A Russian Rediscovers America
10. Adolf Shvedchikov: Parade of Life - poems in English and Russian
11. Adolf Shvedchikov: Overcoming Sorrow - poems in English and Russian
12. Sophia Dediu: Sophia meets Japan
13. Corneliu Leu: Roosevelt, Churchill, Stalin and Hitler: Their surprising role in Eastern Europe in 1944
14. Proceedings of the 5th International Conference "Computational Mechanics and Virtual Engineering" COMEC 2013
15. Georgeta Simion – Potanga: Beyond Imagination: A Thought-provoking novel inspired from mid-20th century events
16. Ana Dediu: The poetry of my life in Europe and The USA
17. Ana Dediu: The Four Graces
18. Proceedings of the 5th International Conference "Advanced Composite Materials Engineering" COMAT 2014
19. Sophia Dediu: Chocolate Cook Book: Is there such a thing as too much chocolate?

20. Sorin Vlase: Mechanical Identifiability in Automotive Engineering
21. Gabriel Dima: The Evolution of the Aerostructures – Concept and Technologies
22. Proceedings of the 6th International Conference "Computational Mechanics and Virtual Engineering" COMEC 2015
23. Sophia Dediu: Cook Book 1 A-B-C Common sense cooking
24. Sophia Dediu: Dim Sum Spring Festival
25. Ana Dediu and Sophia Dediu: Europe in 1985: A chronological and photographic documentary
26 Stefan Staretu: Europe: Serbian Despotate of Srem and the Romanian area. Between the 14th and the 16th Centuries

Chicago (1833): Leo Burnett Building (right, 1989, 46 fl, 193 m), Unitrin Building (2nd from right, 1962, 41 fl, 160 m), 35 East Wacker Drive Building (3rd from right, 1927, 40 fl, 159 m), London Guarantee Bldg. (center-right, 1923, 22 fl, 97 m), the north-east monument (center) of the Michigan Avenue Bridge over Chicago River, 333 North Michigan Bldg. (center-left, 1928, 34 fl, 120 m), Illinois Center (left, 1970, 30 fl, 110 m),

www.ingramcontent.com/pod-product-compliance
Lightning Source LLC
Chambersburg PA
CBHW041606220426
43666CB00001B/4